Also by Julian Baggini

PHILOSOPHY: Key Themes
THE PHILOSOPHER'S TOOLKIT (*with Peter S. Fosl*)
NEW BRITISH PHILOSOPHY: The Interviews (*co-editor with Jeremy Stangroom*)

Philosophy: Key Texts

Julian Baggini

First published 2002 by
PALGRAVE MACMILLAN
Houndmills, Basingstoke, Hampshire RG21 6XS and
175 Fifth Avenue, New York, N.Y. 10010
Companies and representatives throughout the world

PALGRAVE MACMILLAN is the global academic imprint of the Palgrave Macmillan division of St. Martin's Press, LLC and of Palgrave Macmillan Ltd. Macmillan® is a registered trademark in the United States, United Kingdom and other countries. Palgrave is a registered trademark in the European Union and other countries.

ISBN 0–333–96484–5 hardcover
ISBN 0–333–96485–3 paperback

This book is printed on paper suitable for recycling and made from fully managed and sustained forest sources.

A catalogue record for this book is available from the British Library.

Library of Congress Cataloging-in-Publication Data
Baggini, Julian.
    Philosophy : key texts / Julian Baggini.
        p. cm.
    Includes bibliographical references.
    ISBN 0–333–96484–5 — ISBN 0–333–96485–3 (pbk.)
    1. Philosophy.   I. Title.
B72 .B33 2002
100—dc21

                                                                2002025844

10   9   8   7   6   5   4   3   2   1
11   10   09   08   07   06   05   04   03   02

Printed in China

For Beryl and Lino

Contents

2 René Descartes: *Meditations on First Philosophy* (1641)

3 David Hume: *An Enquiry concerning Human Understanding* (1748)

4 Bertrand Russell: *The Problems of Philosophy* (1912)

5 Jean-Paul Sartre: *Existentialism and Humanism* (1947)

Preface

This book is designed to help the reader approach five key works of Western philosophy. It is not a substitute for reading the books themselves, but it will act as a guide for those thinking about or preparing to read or study the books for the first time.

The introduction contains some advice on how to read and make sense of original philosophical texts. Reading philosophy is not like reading a novel and the advice given here should make your encounters with such texts more rewarding.

Each chapter comprises an introduction which sets out the context of the book and its background, a systematic commentary on the text, a summary, a glossary of key terms and suggestions for further reading.

The commentaries combine two main features. First, they summarise and explain the main arguments of each text, clarifying and distilling their core. Second, the commentaries also contain critical points, questioning the validity or soundness of arguments, or bringing out unclarity or ambiguity in the text. The main purpose of this is not to provide an exhaustive catalogue of criticisms which could be made of the text, but to highlight potential weaknesses and to encourage the reader to question the claims being made in the texts for themselves.

There is also a glossary of key philosophical words at the end of the book, along with suggestions for further reading in philosophy.

Acknowledgements

Thanks to Terka Acton, Penny Simmons and the anonymous reader at the publishers who helped make this book possible and then better than it would otherwise have been. Thanks also are due to my students whose feedback on the teaching materials that formed the bases of this book encouraged me to develop them further.

Introduction

Western philosophy has a wonderful literature. The great books of philosophy surely merit inclusion among any collection of the greatest books of humankind. Plato's *Republic* or Descartes's *Meditations* are as important a part of humanity's literature as Shakespeare's *Hamlet* or Chaucer's *Canterbury Tales*.

However, whereas most experiences of education in the English-speaking world would involve exposure to the great poets, playwrights and dramatists, they often do not include any study at all of the great works of philosophy.

This is a double loss. First, it means that we typically end our educations in ignorance of one the most interesting and important strands in our intellectual history. Second, having never picked up a philosophy text in our lives, we find ourselves ill-equipped to make up for this deficiency in the future. If we do pluck up the courage to delve into an original work of philosophy, we often find ourselves baffled, confused and unable to navigate the strange kind of writing we find there.

What exactly is a philosophy text after all? It is usually not instructional. It isn't fiction. It certainly isn't science. Nor is it history. It's not religion either – we are not presented with a complete world-view which is handed down from above. It's something else, something distinctive and often strange.

The main aim of this book is to provide a set of keys which will enable you to pick up, read and make sense of five major texts in the Western philosophical tradition. As well as providing routes into these particular texts, the book should also familiarise you with some of the more general features of philosophical writing, so that many more texts should become approachable and comprehensible. The book is not a substitute for reading the texts themselves (although whether you go on to read any or all of them is entirely your choice, of course). In that sense it is both a menu and a map. As a menu, it allows you to see what the texts have to offer, to taste them first before deciding whether to consume them in their entirety. As a map, it provides guidance on how to navigate through the texts without getting lost.

The main purpose of this introduction is to provide some general advice on how to make your reading of a philosophical text fruitful. I will also say a little about the particular texts chosen.

▶ Styles of reading

In the Western world, although there are still too many people without basic literacy skills, the ability to read is presumed to be something fairly simple, like riding a bike or swimming, that anyone without certain specific disabilities can do. It does not require any special ability or training. It is properly democratic – anyone can do it and though someone may be able to read faster or have a larger vocabulary, the idea that one can read better, worse or just differently than someone else strikes one as a little odd.

But, in fact, different types of writing do demand different styles of reading. For example, I find it quite hard to read poetry. I am aware that to read poetry properly, one needs to attend to features of the writing that one often glosses over, such as the rhythms and sounds of the words. This is very different to when one is reading for information, when one is concerned with what the words mean or what they are telling you to do. Because I don't often read poetry, this style of reading does not come easily to me and as a result I am sure that much of what is good in poetry passes me by.

Reading philosophy also has its particular (though not necessarily unique) style and if one is not used to it, it can be difficult to do. I would identify three characteristic features of an effective reading style for philosophy: it should generally be slow, critical and analytic.

When I say you need to read philosophy slowly, I do not mean that one should generally lengthen the time one takes over each word or the pauses between them. Rather, I mean that reading philosophy often requires one to pause or reread sentences or whole paragraphs. It is not always obvious what the significance or meaning of a particular passage is at first glance. Sometimes, one needs to go back over a passage several times to really grasp what it is getting at. On other occasions one needs to stop and ponder what has just been said, to try and make sense of it in one's own mind. In short, to an unusually high degree, one needs to be thinking carefully about what one is reading to make sure it is being understood. And this means one needs to include a lot of thinking time in one's reading which is in addition to the time it takes to actually read the words on the page.

This is very different to reading a novel, for example, where part of the pleasure can be the narrative pace which pushes one forward to the next page. It is also different to reading something like history, where one may need to reread in order to learn or memorise the content, but not usually because it was hard to understand the first time.

The second characteristic of an effective reading style for philosophy is that one reads critically. By 'critical' I do not mean that one should always be looking to disagree with what is said. Rather, one should be constantly questioning the text, asking whether its assertions are justified, its arguments well-supported or its conclusions credible. Philosophy texts present arguments and we need to decide whether these arguments work, not just whether we agree with the conclusions or whether the author has been persuasive (see the section on arguments below). To do this we should always be testing and questioning what is presented to us.

Finally, one needs to read philosophy analytically. What I mean by this should become clearer when we look at the importance of arguments in philosophical writing. What I essentially mean by this is that as one reads one should be trying to see how the various parts of the text fit together, how conclusions are derived from premises and how one part of the text supports or disagrees with other parts. What one is analysing here is the way in which the various claims and arguments of the book fit together. Only by doing this can we make sense of the whole of the text. If we cannot do this, we will see in the text only a series of unrelated, unsupported claims.

I have already talked at several points about the role of argument in philosophy texts. We need now to examine this feature of philosophical writing more closely.

▶ Arguments

An argument in philosophy is not a row or dispute, but simply an attempt to establish a conclusion on a rational basis. The simplest forms of argument are three-line inferences known as syllogisms, an example of which is:

1 No dogs have wings.
2 Rufus has wings.
3 Therefore, Rufus is not a dog.

Syllogisms are examples of *deductive* arguments. They have two premises (lines 1 and 2 above), from which a conclusion (line 3) is derived. In a *valid* deductive argument, the truth of the conclusion follows as a matter of necessity from the truth of the premises. Put another way, if the premises are true, the conclusion then *must* be true.

In the example above, we can see that this is a valid deductive argument. If it is true that no dogs have wings and it is true that Rufus has wings, then it must be true that Rufus is not a dog. The vital thing to note here is that we are saying the conclusion must be true *if* the premises are true. One can never tell if the conclusion of a deductive argument *is* actually true unless one knows that the premises are true *and* that the argument is valid. If both these conditions obtain, we say the argument is *sound*.

How do we know if the premises are true? There is no simple answer to this. Some premises will have been established by other arguments. But eventually, we have to end up with premises that are not themselves conclusions of other arguments. Sometimes, this will be because there is evidence from experience that the premises are true. For instance, experience does seem to suggest that no dogs have wings. On other occasions, it may be because the premise is what we might call self-evidently true. Do we really need any proof, for example, that $1 + 1 = 2$? Isn't that obviously true? On other occasions a premise may be true by definition. 'A widow is a woman whose husband has died' is true just because of what those words all mean.

This touches on major issues in philosophy and in the texts discussed in this book, we will see several attempts to pinpoint the types of premises which can function as fundamental truths, which do not need to be proved themselves. We need not consider this further here, but should simply note that arguments have to start from somewhere.

Deductive arguments are the most rigorous form of argument and there are basically two ways of finding fault with them. The first is to find that they are not valid: in other words, that the conclusion does not necessarily follow from the premises. For example:

1   Jack studies the Qur'an.
2   Muslims study the Qur'an.
3   Therefore, Jack is a Muslim.

This is invalid because the premises (lines 1 and 2) might both be true, but the conclusion (line 3) could still be false. For example, Jack may be Jewish and reading the Qur'an because he is a student of comparative religion. This means the truth of the premises does not guarantee the truth of the conclusion, so the argument is not valid.

There is a second way in which arguments can be found wanting. Consider this example:

1   Jack studies the Qur'an.
2   Only Muslims study the Qur'an.
3   Therefore, Jack is a Muslim.

In this case, the argument is valid. If it is true that Jack is studying the Qur'an and if it is true that only Muslims study the Qur'an, then Jack must be a Muslim. But, of course, it is not true that only Muslims study the Qur'an. This means that although the argument is valid, it is not sound since one of its premises is false.

Note that in an unsound or an invalid argument the conclusion can be true. It might be the case that Jack is a Muslim. But both arguments are still inadequate because they do not *establish* that he is a Muslim. In other words, the 'therefore' that precedes the conclusion is not justified: it is not because of what has been said in the premises that the conclusion is true.

When you come to read actual philosophical texts, you will rarely see arguments set out in the form above. What we have done so far is looked at schematised, idealised, stripped-down versions of arguments. In actual philosophical texts, things are not so simple. However, understanding the basic principles which govern simple deductive arguments like the ones above will help you to make sense of and assess arguments in actual philosophical works. This is because all works of philosophy essentially put forward arguments. So how do you apply what we have said about arguments to these texts?

▶ Assessing premises

First of all, in any philosophical text there are some beliefs, sentences or propositions which function as the premises. You need to look for these if you are to understand how the argument works and whether it is valid or sound. When looking for premises, you are looking for the beliefs which form the bases of the arguments.

For example, in Sartre's *Existentialism and Humanism*, you will find that many of his arguments are based on the premise that human beings have free will. In Descartes's *Meditations*, you will find that one basic premise is that a thing's essence is that which it cannot be conceived without. In *Hume's Enquiry concerning Human Understanding*, you will find that one premise is that all we are directly aware of are the contents of our own minds.

Having identified these premises, you then need to consider on what grounds they stand. In Hume's case, for example, the premise is based on experience. To see if the premise is true, one therefore has to decide if what Hume says corresponds to experience. In Descartes's case, it seems that his basic premise about essences is not based on experience, but is somehow taken to be self-evidently true. In this case, one needs to decide if it really is self-evident or whether such a premise should in fact be based in experience. In Sartre's case, we need to consider on what grounds we can say we are in fact free. It is not clear why Sartre thinks this is so basic as to not require any proof or demonstration, but as readers we can consider for ourselves whether his premise is admissible.

As these examples show, once we are attuned to the idea that a philosophical text will be offering us arguments and that arguments rest on premises, we can begin to look for these premises in the text, consider the adequacy of the support they are given in the text, and also assess them independently of the text, bringing our own doubts or considerations to bear on them. We can also distinguish between what the argument rests on and what the argument aims to show, which is its conclusion.

▶ Inferences

Having distinguished the premises and the conclusions, we can then try to examine the argumentative link between them. Has the philosopher in question demonstrated that the conclusion does necessarily follow from the premises? If they do not, is this because of a small error that we can rectify or are the flaws more fundamental? In order to make such a judgement we must understand what a valid deduction looks like.

However, there are more ways of moving from premises to conclusion than just deduction. One such method is induction. This is where we use the evidence of the past or present to reach conclusions about things we are not able to observe, in the past, present or future.

Such arguments often look like deductive arguments. For example:

1 Mary claimed to have run 100 metres in eight seconds.
2 No woman has ever run 100 metres in less than ten seconds.
3 Therefore, Mary is lying.

Superficially, this looks like a deductive argument. But as a deductive argument, it fails. The fact that no one has ever done what Mary claims to have done (or even come close) does not guarantee that Mary is lying. A deductive argument is only valid if the truth of the premises guarantees the truth of the conclusion and this is not what happens here. Does this mean the argument fails?

Not necessarily. This argument should be read as an inductive argument, not as a deductive one. Here, the evidence of experience (that no woman has run 100 metres in under ten seconds) is being used to support a conclusion (Mary is lying) which we cannot verify by any direct observation or application of pure logic. In such an argument the movement from premises to conclusion has logical gaps. But there are many times when this kind of reasoning is all we can go on. It is this kind of reasoning, for example, that enables us to predict that if I let go of a ball, it will drop rather than float away. Unless we can use our general experience as a guide to what we have not experienced, we are unable to function in the world.

So when evaluating an argument, one might find that it is deductively unsound. But then you need to consider whether it is the type of argument where inductive justifications are more appropriate. If it is, you need to use more judgement in your assessment of the argument, because the rules for the correct use of an inductive argument are not as clear-cut as those for deduction. You need to ask whether experience provides enough evidence to support the conclusion and there is no generally accepted formula for deciding what is enough.

One other way of justifying the inference from premises to conclusion is by a method known as abduction, or 'argument to best explanation'. This is pretty much self-explanatory and a simple example will help make it clear. Consider, as Bertrand Russell does in *The Problems of Philosophy*, the question of whether or not our perceptions of things are caused by objects independent of us or whether they are just figments of our imaginations. It is no good appealing to experience to solve this one, since what is being countenanced is the possibility that experience is itself misleading. One cannot appeal to what is in dispute to settle the dispute. So how do we resolve this issue?

Russell employs abduction to solve the conundrum. If things do exist independently of us, then this explains why there is so much regularity in our experiences, why things are generally where we left them and so on. It also explains why we are not in total control of our environment; rather, our environment constrains us in many ways. If, on the other hand, we were dreaming all this, why would our experiences be so regular and orderly? Why wouldn't things happen spontaneously, without cause, as they do in dreams? Why are we unable to control things just by our own powers of thought?

When we compare the two possibilities, therefore, we see that one just offers a better explanation than another. In that situation, I am justified in concluding that the better explanation is probably the true one. As with induction, there are no hard and fast rules for determining what a better explanation is like. Some judgement is required.

Deduction, induction and abduction are three different forms of reasoning. But all have in common a pattern of movement from premises to conclusions based on an appropriate and acceptable method of inference. When reading a philosophical text, you don't just need to be able to identify the premises and conclusions – you also need to be able to identify and assess the way in which the writer argues to the conclusions from their premises.

▶ The archaeology of arguments

Assessing arguments in the way described is not always easy. Sometimes, the structure and form of an argument are very clear. But on other occasions it takes some concentrated thought to tease out the premises, the conclusions and their relations. Conclusions are easier to spot, because they tend to be preceded by words and phrases such as 'therefore', 'it follows that', 'thus' or 'hence'. Premises, however, can be very elusive.

Indeed, sometimes premises can go entirely unstated. This tends to be the case when an argument rests upon an assumption that perhaps even the author herself does not realise she is making. For example, Descartes's *Meditations* seems to be premised on the assumption that something that cannot be doubted must be true. Descartes never directly justifies this assumption, but it does seem to underlie a lot of his arguments.

Having dug up a premise like this, we can then scrutinise it to see if it stands up. In this case, we might conclude it does not. After all, whether we can doubt something or not surely only tells us about our own capacity for credulity. Isn't it more than possible that we can doubt things that are true as easily as we can find it impossible to doubt what is in fact false?

Often, it is when one engages in this kind of archaeology that one ends up making the most telling criticisms. The weakest premises are often those which the writer herself has failed to realise require justification. This is because such premises are often mere assumptions, and it is always dangerous in philosophy to assume anything.

▶ Arguments within arguments

An argument is like a little mechanism which produces conclusions from premises. The great works of philosophy often contain many such small mechanisms, all working together as part of a larger, single mechanism. In order to properly understand such a text, one therefore needs not only to be able to see how each individual argument works, but how they all fit together into the bigger picture.

One of the greatest examples of this is Descartes's *Meditations*. Zoom out and you can see how the book fits together as one, single argument. It moves from a systematic doubt of all assumed knowledge, through to the establishment of a certain foundation for knowledge, and then carefully builds on these foundations until an entire edifice of knowledge is completed. It is a remarkable text and one can see how each meditation advances the argument forward to its next stage.

But if one stays with this overview, one misses the many crucial details. In order to properly assess the overarching argument of the *Meditations*, one needs to zoom in to look at the various smaller arguments contained in each meditation. The momentum which moves the whole book forward is ultimately created by these small arguments.

Further, these arguments often depend upon each other. Often the conclusion of one argument becomes a premise for another, moving through the book like something on a factory assembly line. In isolation, an argument may appear baseless. But when one looks at what has come before, one can sometimes find its proper foundation. In isolation, an argument can also look trivial or uninteresting.

Only when you can see why the conclusion it generates is needed elsewhere can you properly understand its significance.

One can see, then, that in order to be able to read a philosophy text properly, one must be able to zoom in and out in this way. One needs to be able to look at each individual argument and see how it works, but one also needs to see how each argument fits into the whole.

▶ Back to style

Returning to my earlier comments about styles of reading, we can now see more clearly why it needs to be slow, critical and analytic. If one is to identify and uncover premises, identify and assess the mode of inference which leads to the conclusions, and see how everything fits together into the bigger picture, there is a lot one needs to actually be doing other than merely taking in the words on the page. For this reason, reading philosophy is best understood as a special kind of activity, unlike much other reading.

This activity cannot be performed properly if the reading is done too quickly. It is only possible to pick out and identify all the relevant parts and relations of the arguments if they are read analytically. And one is not going to be able to make fair assessments if one is not reading critically.

▶ The principle of charity

Many people find that part of the fun of reading philosophy is learning to spot bad arguments. Discovering an invalid deduction or a questionable premise can be a great pleasure, especially when it allows us to think that we have out-smarted one of the greats.

I wouldn't want to suggest that this pleasure should never be indulged, but when seeking it becomes the primary motivation for reading a philosophy text, much of what is of value in philosophy is lost. In general we should remember that it is easier to demolish than to build. We are no more the equals of Aristotle, Descartes, Hume, Russell and Sartre because we can find faults in the arguments than we are the equals of the great artists because we can spot flaws in their paintings.

But it is not the inflation of the ego which is the main risk when we read philosophy mainly to demolish it. The main victim tends to be understanding itself. Texts often need to be interpreted and they can be interpreted in ways which show them in a better or worse light. If we spot what we think is a glaring error, we should not be triumphalist. Rather, we should ask whether the writer really did make this mistake or whether they have in some way already anticipated it.

Even if it does seem that the philosopher has slipped up, the next stage should be to see whether the error can be remedied rather than gloating over the failure of the argument. Often, adjustments can be made to a philosopher's position to accommodate criticisms, adjustments which preserve the essential nature of the position being argued for. We should consider whether this is possible before we reject the philosopher's position as flawed.

Such a warning is necessary because, unfortunately, much philosophical education seems to be based on the principle that arguments are put up as target practice for students to practice their skills of intellectual demolition. This is without doubt good for honing certain philosophical skills. But a reader who only learns the negative skills of demolition is unlikely to develop the wisdom and insight necessary to get the most out of their philosophising.

In short, it is good practice to employ the principle of charity: always try and interpret an argument in the way which makes it stronger, not weaker. That way you are more likely to hit upon the truth.

▶ Five key texts

The five books selected for this volume represent a broad spread of philosophy's great literature. Three are indisputably classics: Aristotle's *Ethics*, Descartes's *Meditations* and Hume's *Enquiry*. Anyone wishing to read the best works of Western philosophy would be advised to include these texts in their libraries. Sartre's *Existentialism and Humanism* and Russell's *The Problems of Philosophy* are different kinds of beasts. Russell and Sartre are two of the most important philosophers of the twentieth century, though they represent two divergent traditions: the Anglo-American 'analytic' school and the Franco-German 'phenomenological' school. (Be warned that these labels, though helpful, undoubtedly simplify and exaggerate the differences.) Their own master works are the *Principia Mathematica* and *Being and Nothingness* respectively. Both these texts are, however, inaccessible to the beginner in philosophy. For this reason, the best way into the thought of these great thinkers is through the books they wrote themselves for a wider readership.

Having read this book slowly, critically and analytically, my hope is that you will be able to read the original texts themselves in exactly the same way.

1 Aristotle: *The Nicomachean Ethics* (*c.*334–323 BCE)

▶ Background

The history of Western thought has been summed up by Alfred North White-head as 'footnotes to Plato'. One of the first great philosophers to add his own footnotes was Aristotle, though the sheer breadth, originality and distinctiveness of his work makes a mockery of any attempt to see his writings as mere append-ages to Plato's.

Aristotle wrote on subjects we would today call philosophy, linguistics, biology, political science, literary theory, cosmology and others. He studied in Plato's Academy in Athens, briefly becoming tutor to Alexander the Great before returning to Athens to set up the Lyceum, an institute of learning in the mould of the Academy.

Plato and Aristotle embody an essential difference in how the philosophical enterprise is conceived. In Plato we see the search for eternal truths, for certainty, for precision and for the reality behind the appearance of the world. Aristotle in many ways shares these aims. But they are tempered by what one might call a realism or pragmatism. For Aristotle, the quest for knowledge has to start with what we have got, imperfect though it may be. We also have to accept that we may not be able to achieve absolute certainty and that absolute pre-cision may also be impossible in some enquiries. And though we do want to uncover the truths that lie behind appearances, these may still be truths of our world, rather than of some mystical other realm, which Plato often seems to imply.

In this way, Aristotle is an example of a very worldly philosopher, while Plato is an other-worldly one. While many see wisdom in Aristotle's realism and fantasy in Plato's grander projects, others see Aristotle as lacking in ambition and Plato as representing the purer philosophical impulse.

Aristotle's reputation has certainly fluctuated according to the philosophical fashions of the time. In Europe, Aristotle did not come into eminence until the thirteenth century and by 1500 he was out of fashion again. Only in the nine-teenth century did he re-remerge, acknowledged as a pivotal figure in the history of philosophy.

▶ The text

What we now read as the works of Aristotle are generally not much more than lecture notes. They were certainly not written as books. In the case of the *Nicomachean Ethics* (or just the *Ethics* for short), this does not make the text more difficult to read. If anything, the short sections into which the book is often arranged make the text easier to read than many philosophical tracts, since each major new point is clearly demarcated.

The *Ethics* is longer than the other four texts discussed in this book. For this reason, I focus my discussion on five of its ten books: Books 1, 2, 3, 6 and 10. My discussion is arranged according to themes, in the order in which they are introduced in the book. This means that although the commentary follows the order of the book, I will at times leap forward to later passages directly related to the section being discussed. My references are to the pages on Bekker's Greek text, which are standardly used to identify passages in Aristotle and are found in any good translation.

Readers should bear in mind that many of Aristotle's original Greek terms can only be approximately rendered in English. At times I have used the original Greek words, but where I haven't one should be mindful that what Aristotle meant may not be exactly what the English equivalent means.

▶ The proper method of philosophy

As I suggested above, one of the keys to understanding Aristotle is to understand how he viewed philosophy. Reading the great works in the history of philosophy, it is possible to discern three different ways of approaching the subject.

One approach, exemplified in Plato, Descartes and Spinoza, is to see philosophy as fundamentally an *a priori* discipline. Reasoning is *a priori* if it is based on deductions from what are usually called first principles. These first principles are not observations about the nature of the world, but self-evident truths of logic, mathematics and language. The idea of *a priori* reasoning is that from basic truths such as 'nothing can both be and not be' and 'every effect must have a cause', we can deduce all the other important truths about the world. The method of deduction to be used is as precise and rigorous as that of mathematics. If one sees philosophy as an *a priori* discipline, then, one believes that straight thinking alone is enough to answer all the important questions of philosophy.

In contrast, other philosophers, notably the British empiricists Locke, Berkeley and Hume, see philosophy as largely an *a posteriori* discipline. This means that they believe philosophical reasoning is based on the findings of experience, not first principles. It is not our faculty of reason operating alone which allows us to discover the nature of the world, but our reason combined with the lessons of experience. Further, our reasoning cannot always follow the model of mathematical deduction. Often, we have to be satisfied with something less precise.

Within this *a posteriori* tradition there are two sub-divisions. On the one hand, there are those that see philosophy as being akin to science. Philosophy may not have the rigour and methods of mathematics, but it has the different rigour and methods of science. The alternative is to see philosophy as what one might call a humanistic discipline. On this view, philosophy is not like science or maths. Rather, it is an attempt to make sense of, understand and describe the human condition in ways which make sense to humans themselves. Maths, with its abstractions, and science, with its detachment from human concerns and perspectives, are both inadequate to deal with philosophy's key problems. What we gain from their rigour we lose in their inability to address the human concerns of philosophy.

So we can see that philosophers tend to view their subject as mainly *a priori*, scientistic or humanistic. The amazing thing about Aristotle is that he cannot be pigeonholed into any one of these three categories. Aristotle's wisdom was to see that which approach you take depends entirely on what question you are addressing. In his writings on logic, for example, he is as *a prioristic* as any philosopher. In the *Ethics*, on the other hand, he accepts that a different approach is needed. 'It is a mark of the trained mind never to expect more precision in the treatment of any subject than the nature of that subject permits', he wrote (1094b).

Aristotle describes the subject matter of the *Ethics* as politics: 'the science that studies the supreme good for man' (1094b). It is best here to accept this definition and not get confused by thinking of our modern use of the word 'politics'. At several points Aristotle notes that politics is not an exact science and that, as a result, we can only form general rules about it. We would be doomed to failure if we tried to come up with very specific rules for human conduct. In this way, we can see that in the *Ethics*, Aristotle adopts a broadly *a posteriori* approach. But one needs to be aware that Aristotle is supremely flexible in his methodology. At times we can see examples of *a priori*, scientistic and humanistic approaches in this text. It's very much a case of selecting the right intellectual tool for the job. So in judging the success or failure of Aristotle's arguments, one question that one always needs to ask is whether he has chosen the right instrument.

▶ Teleology

One of the most significant passages in the *Ethics* comes right at the start (1094a). This is where Aristotle sets out the basic presupposition which underlies his whole enquiry. The passage is, however, brief, and one needs to relate it to Aristotle's broader philosophy to see its full significance.

The key concept here – though it doesn't appear in the text – is that of 'teleology'. This has its root in the Greek word *telos*, meaning end or goal. It is one of Aristotle's most famous – or perhaps notorious – ideas that one best understands the nature of any thing by looking at its end, goal or purpose. (As none of these words by itself quite captures the full meaning, I'll sometimes continue to use *telos*.) For example, the *telos* of a knife is to cut, and it is only by seeing that a knife serves this end or function that one can really understand what a knife is. In the world of nature, the *telos* of an eye is to see, the *telos* of a giraffe's long neck is to allow it to reach high vegetation and so on.

Aristotle clearly believed he was on to something with this idea for he extended it to encompass all forms of human activity. So, for instance, the *telos* of medicine is the end or purpose to which medicine is dedicated – good health; the *telos* of warfare is what warfare aims for – victory; and the *telos* of business is the purpose it serves – the creation of wealth.

If you now consider how the various ends and goals of human activity fit together, you can easily see that some are subordinate to others. For example, my goal in working may be to earn money, but I may only wish to earn money because I want to be able to afford a decent house. So here, the *telos* of earning money is subordinate to the *telos* of owning a good house. This would be confirmed were I to agree that, if I had to choose between having a lot of money in the bank or having a good home, I'd take the good home.

In more everyday language, the basic thought is that we do many things as means to an end and some of these ends are, in the bigger picture, means to other, more important ends. In Aristotelian language, all activities have their own *telos*, but these may themselves be means of achieving a more fundamental *telos*.

It's quite obvious that, if this is true, then eventually we have to reach a point where the end really is the end. If everything turned out to be a means to an end, that would mean nothing was worth doing or having in itself. So eventually, we have to end up with something which is valuable in itself, something which is the ultimate end, the ultimate *telos* of human activity.

This final or supreme *telos* Aristotle calls the Good. It's important to note that the Good is not some kind of weird, mystical entity, like Plato's form of the Good. Rather, the Good is just whatever turns out to be the ultimate *telos* of human life. One purpose of the *Ethics* is to discover what this Good is, so Aristotle is certainly not suggesting it must be forever shrouded in mystery.

Aristotle's teleological approach is very appealing, but it is not without its problems. First of all, as a principle in science it seems to get things the wrong way around. According to evolutionary theory, you understand why giraffes have long necks and animals have eyes not by looking at what their purpose is, but by examining the evolutionary mechanisms which led them to come into exist-ence. For example, giraffes have long necks because, over thousands of years, giraffes with longer necks have been more successful at reaching foliage and thus staying alive than their shorter necked peers. Hence, longer necked giraffes are more likely to survive and have offspring that also have long necks. This process of natural selection means that, over time, giraffes have evolved into a long-necked species. It is certainly not the case that giraffes decided in some strange way to grow longer necks or their necks were designed in order to serve the *telos* of reaching high foliage.

In the ethical sphere, perhaps the greatest problem for Aristotle is that it is not clear why we should think there is one *telos* for all human activity. One possibility is that there is a plurality of ends which are all worth pursuing and that our activity may be divided between pursuing any number of them. Another possibility, argued for by Sartre (see Chapter 5 on *Existentialism and Humanism*), is that there is no pre-set *telos* for mankind. Rather, each individual needs to decide their own goals or ends. The idea of a single end or goal may help us to understand objects and animals, but perhaps it is too limited a way of looking at human life.

▶ The Good for human life

If Aristotle is right and there is a supreme Good, a goal or end for human life, then what is it? Aristotle certainly has some clear ideas about what it is not. Pleasure cannot be the end of human life, says Aristotle, but to fully understand why he says this, we need to consider how he viewed pleasure, which we will do in the section on the role of pleasure.

Aristotle also thought that public honour could not be the supreme Good. If public honour sounds like an odd candidate for the ultimate end of human life, then one should remember that public honour means more or less the same as fame. We know in our own age the great attraction fame holds. Many people desire above all else to be famous. Indeed, there are people who are not famous for being anything in particular, they are just famous for being famous. People will do all sorts of things for fame, even the meagre '15 minutes of fame' that is offered by appearing on a TV game show.

But fame is rejected by Aristotle as the ultimate end. First, it is just too ephemeral and transitory. We know how today's cover-star is tomorrow's yesterday's man. The 'where are they now?' columns of popular magazines testify to that. Perhaps more importantly, Aristotle notes that 'honour is felt to depend more on those who confer than on him who receives it' (1095b). There is a sense here that the ultimate end of life must be something which is internal to the individual: if you have achieved the ultimate goal of life, then that should depend on who you are and what you have done, not on how others happen to see you. This sounds plausible, but maybe this view excludes the possibility that in this sphere life just isn't fair, and whether you achieve the ultimate end in life may well depend on others. We may feel it *should* depend on us and us alone, but the world is not commanded by such shoulds.

There is a third possibility: the contemplative life, which we will look at in the next section on happiness.

To recapitulate, the ultimate end of human life, which we can call the Good for humanity, must be something which is good in itself and is not merely a means to an end. There is one thing which fits this description: happiness. What exactly happiness is is discussed in the next section. For now, we only need to note that happiness is indeed the one thing which is considered good in itself and is never valued for some other reason other than its own goodness.

There is a further condition Aristotle places on the Good: it must be self-sufficient (1097b). In other words, if one possesses the ultimate Good, that should be enough. It should be complete and one should not need anything else. At this point one might object that happiness does sometimes depend on other things. For example, being in a good relationship may make you happy, but then your happiness is dependent on someone else and so it is not self-sufficient. You might also think that happiness depends on having a certain amount of money, which again stops it being self-sufficient.

However, these objections are too quick. At this stage Aristotle is merely sketching out what the human Good is. He hasn't yet provided the details. The conclusion so far is that it must be a kind of self-sufficient happiness. What precisely this is comes later and it may well be that the kind of happiness we get from relationships and money doesn't fit the bill. In that case, the response might be, 'So much for relationships and money', rather than, 'So much for Aristotle's theory'.

At this point, Aristotle makes a further addition to his definition of the Good which comes from a rather different direction. So far, his approach has been broadly humanistic. That is to say, his enquiry has been based on general considerations about what makes a human life go well from a human perspective. Now, however, his thought takes a scientistic turn. Aristotle adopts a general principle that one needs to understand the distinctive function of a thing in order to understand its essence. In the case of human activities, we only understand what a pianist is, for example, if we understand that their distinctive function is to play the piano. Further, a good pianist is one who performs this function well.

This general principle also applies to biology. The distinctive function of plant life is nutrition and growth. Animals also need nourishment and grow, but this is not what distinguishes animals since this is something they share with plants. Animals also have sentience: a consciousness or awareness of the world about them and perhaps even of themselves. Sentience, then, is the distinctive function of animals. Humans need nourishment, grow and have sentience, but in addition they have the unique (according to Aristotle) capacity to reason. So rational thought is the distinctive function of humanity.

Just as being a good pianist means performing the distinctive function of the pianist well, so Aristotle believes being a good person means performing the distinctive function of being a person well. This means that the Good implies activity: it is not a state of being, but is the living of life according to the proper function of humanity. The conclusion therefore is that the Good for humans is living a life in accordance with rational principles.

In J. A. K. Thomson's translation of Aristotle's language this means the Good is 'an activity of the soul in accordance with virtue'. To modern ears, this is deceptive. By 'soul' Aristotle does not mean some kind of immaterial, ghostly substance. Soul is rather the way in which an individual organism is structured in order to fulfil its function. Similarly, 'virtue' has a moralistic air to it that is not always appropriate to Aristotle. We are better to think of virtue as human excellence which allows us to perform our function well (see 1106a). Hence, we can see that the rather ephemeral sounding 'virtuous activity of the soul' is really nothing more than the living of life in the way best suited to our natures as rational beings.

So we now have an account of the Good for humans which incorporates several features. First, the Good is happiness. Second, this Good life is self-sufficient. Third, this Good can only be achieved by living our lives according to our proper function as rational beings. These three conditions are necessary and sufficient for the Good life. That is to say, we need all of them in order to achieve the Good, none can be dispensed with and together they are complete.

This definition also explains how we come by happiness: by living virtuously in accordance with our proper function. In this way, the different components of the good life cannot be entirely separated out: one only understands a single part of it when one sees how it fits into the whole. Indeed, the word Aristotle uses for happiness – *eudaimonia* – is often translated as 'human flourishing'. This captures better than 'happiness' the way in which the good life requires us to live lives to the full, according to our essential nature as rational beings.

To support this account, Aristotle looks at what other wise sages have said about the good life and is pleased to report that their views support his (1098b). This kind of appeal to general wisdom is distinctive of Aristotle's approach to many philosophical issues. Wisdom about the Good for humankind is something one finds mainly in humanistic discourse, rather than scientific and *a priori* reasoning. Therefore, to look to the opinions of admired colleagues and predecessors seems a natural way of testing whether one's own thoughts chime with the wisdom of the ages. However, there is a twinge of the scientific about this, at least a hint of social science. Aristotle argues that if his view is correct, it will be found to be in harmony with established facts. This could also be said of any scientific theory. What is different is that the facts in question here are other people's opinions.

▶ Happiness

Aristotle has a lot more to say about happiness and its part in the good life. One interesting feature of his discussion is that, in it, Aristotle shows a worldliness and realism often lacking in philosophical accounts of the good life. For example, he admits that a minimum amount of wealth is required to live the good life, for without this, one's ability to live properly is hindered by material constraints. He also acknowledges that good or bad fortune plays a part, saying that one's place in society or even one's looks can have an effect on one's happiness.

None the less, he is a little equivocal on this matter, for he also says 'that the most important and finest thing of all should be left to chance would be a gross disharmony' (1100a). Aristotle, while accepting luck plays a part, also believes that happiness can be cultivated, learned or acquired. By living life well according to our true function, we will become happy. If, however, we live like beasts or plants, only concerned for growth, nutrition or sensual pleasures, then we will inevitably fail to achieve proper happiness. So, although luck plays a part, behaviour and habit is even more important.

One might feel that this is all a bit too vague. Just how much is down to luck and how much is down to our own efforts? While such questions are perhaps understandable, we must remember what Aristotle says about this subject he calls politics: It is not an exact science. One can do no better than state generalities. We may be able to find examples of people who behave impeccably yet end up unhappy due to misfortune; or even cases of people coming by happiness by pure chance, despite not living well at all. Such exceptions to the rule are bound to crop up every now and again. Aristotle can do no more than come up with general guidelines: follow this path and nine times out of ten you'll be happy. Fail to do so and nine times out of ten you won't. This is no more vague and unsatisfactory than dietary advice which says that women on average need 2000 calories a day to be healthy and men 2500. The fact that some men can readily get by on much less than 2000 calories and some women need more than 2500 in no way undermines the truth of the general claim.

If this seems unsatisfactory, then so might what Aristotle says about death and happiness. Here Aristotle is confronted by a seeming paradox. The problem is this: can we call a person happy before they have died? The answer may obviously seem to be yes. But now consider the example of a woman who has lived what seems to be a full and happy life. Shortly before her death, however, she suffers great misfortunes, including the death of her children. Further, she discovers things which entirely change how she views the past. For instance, having thought she had lived in a loving, honest and faithful marriage she discovers that, in fact, her husband has been conducting a long-standing affair with another woman. We would not say that this woman's life as a whole was happy, but we would not be in a position to say this until the very end when events turned her life upside down.

One can also imagine an example in which the opposite is the case. Someone might live a life where for many years they struggle and are unhappy but finally, shortly before death, they reach fulfilment and their life is somehow redeemed. We would not say this person had lived a miserable life.

So it seems that we cannot say whether a person is truly happy until we have seen how their whole life pans out. But Aristotle has said that happiness is a kind of activity. So it can only surely be when one is engaged in that activity, when one is still alive, that one can say whether a person is happy.

Aristotle's solution is to argue that the truly happy person can never become really miserable because they will be able to bear misfortunes with equanimity. It is true that we need to look at a person's whole life, but if they are truly good, then we can be confident that they will be happy until the end. If we elaborate on what Aristotle actually says, we can perhaps see this solution as turning on a distinction between what *constitutes* happiness and what we can *know about* happiness. A person is happy if they are living virtuously in this life, and if they are indeed living in this way, they will remain happy until their death. But we may not be able to know whether a person is truly happy until their death because it is hard to say whether the way a person seems to be is a true reflection of their 'soul'.

But what about after death? Can the fortunes of your descendents or changes in your reputation have an impact on you? Aristotle says it would be heartless to deny it. But this seems to go against his view that happiness is a kind of activity, if it can be affected by things that happen when you are no longer active! Aristotle accepts that what happens after your death can have some effect, but he says that it cannot transform the happy person into an unhappy one or vice versa. This is perhaps too quick a concession to popular belief, for it seems that nothing in the good life – virtuous activity which produces a kind of self-contained happiness – can be affected by what happens after that life is finished.

Aristotle ties up his discussion of happiness right at the end of the *Ethics* in Book 10 (1176b). He recapitulates the key idea that happiness is a kind of activity rather than a state and he also draws the distinction between happiness and amusement or pleasure. While the latter can be enjoyed by anyone or any beast, they do not give the deep and sustainable happiness that a life lived virtuously can.

The main interest in this recapitulation, however, is what Aristotle says about the role of contemplation in happiness (1177a). In the earlier parts of the book he says that happiness is a virtuous activity of the soul in accordance with a rational principle, but he doesn't say much about the specific role of thought in happiness.

Contemplation is thought to be the surest route to happiness because the intellect is our highest faculty. Remember that plants grow, animals have experiences, but only humans think. Thus, thinking is what sets us above them and it is in our capacity to think that we find our highest and most distinctly human nature.

Intellectual pursuits also have advantages over many others. First, they are self-sufficient. Whereas the pleasures of, say, fine wine, depend on having a well-stocked cellar, all one needs is a good brain to have a good think. Also, thinking has as its goal only more and better thoughts, so it is something which is done for its own sake, in contrast to many other pursuits where getting hold of something else is the goal. Unlike practical activities, contemplation is something one does when one is at leisure for its own sake.

This makes contemplation superior even to moral activity. In one's dealings with others one does not find the purity and self-sufficiency of intellectual life. To act justly or generously requires feeling and material resources, both of which are more tied to our animal nature than pure contemplation.

Some readers may find something self-serving about Aristotle's stress on intellectual contemplation as the highest form of happiness. 'Philosophy is held to entail pleasures that are marvellous in purity and permanence', he writes. He also says that in intellectual contemplation we share something of the divine. Can we be sure that Aristotle is valuing philosophy so highly because he likes it, rather than because it is the highest form of activity? There is certainly something implausible in the idea that intellectual contemplation is the surest route to happiness for all people. Artists and musicians, as well as those who enjoy art and music, may get their highest pleasures not from intellectual contemplation, but from aesthetic experience. We might also question why Aristotle values the solitary nature of contemplation over the social nature of moral activity. Is this any more than a preference for the private over the public realm? There is a serious doubt here that Aristotle has focused too much on what he finds dear, not on what all mankind should value as the highest good.

▶ Moral virtue

Although Aristotle argues that intellectual virtues are the highest, he does not think that moral virtues are unimportant. Far from it: much of the *Ethics* is concerned with these moral virtues.

There is one very important difference between moral and intellectual virtues. Intellect is something which one improves by practice, instruction and learning. Moral virtue, in contrast, is developed by habit (1103a) and is considered to be a disposition rather then a feeling or a faculty (1105b). This is one of the most enduring and distinctive features of Aristotelian ethics. Aristotle's great insight is that, when it comes to behaving well or badly (or as Aristotle often puts it, justly or unjustly), we are more than anything creatures of habit. For example, imagine there is a fire in a house and two people are in a position to try and save the inhabitants, but at great personal risk. One is courageous by habit. The other has never been brave, but is good at moral philosophy. Which is more likely to be brave and help the people inside? Surely it would the person for whom bravery comes naturally. Or, to take a different example, what of the reactions of two people when confronted with a person in financial need, one of whom has cultivated the habit of generosity and the other who does not habitually give money away, but on rational reflection might decide it is a good thing to help out? Again, it seems that the habitually generous person is the one most likely to do the right thing.

Obviously, for Aristotle there is a role for rationality in ethics. First, one has to decide which attitudes and habits to develop and which to suppress. Second, one needs to be able to do a bit of thinking on the spot to avoid being rash instead of brave, or wasteful instead of generous. But, nevertheless, it is still true that if we are to live well, we need to develop our characters so that behaving well comes naturally, or else reason will be powerless to overcome our habits.

We should be careful not to attribute to Aristotle the crude view that the just person is simply the person who performs just acts. He is aware that someone may do the right thing by accident (1105a). The truly just person, in contrast not only does the right thing, but does it because she knows it is the right thing, has chosen to do it for no other reason than that it is the right thing, and she does so because her character is a stable and good one.

To see why all these three conditions must obtain, consider what happens when one is missing in a case of doing something good, like giving money to the poor. If a person is in general a good person and chooses to give some money, but doesn't know that they are giving it to the poor, then they are being good by accident. Similarly, if they are a good person and give money to the poor, but don't do so voluntarily or do so because they will get some kind of reward, then again they are only being good by accident.

But what of the third possibility, a person whose character is bad but who gives to the poor voluntarily, for no other reason than it is good to do so, knowing it is the right thing. Why is that considered only accidentally good by Aristotle? Perhaps the reason is this. Such a person is not in general good. Their momentary desire to do good is not the result of a fixed and settled disposition. This means that they acted 'out of character'. When a person acts in such a way, there is a sense in which this is a kind of accident. It is as though, for no apparent reason, one starts to behave differently. If one is not in control of this change of character and one soon reverts to one's old ways, then it does seem to be true that in some sense it is just accidental that one behaves well on this occasion. It was not the result of any kind of decision or training on the agent's part.

If one is to lead this virtuous life, one obviously needs to learn how to behave virtuously. To do this, one needs to understand one of Aristotle's most famous principles: the doctrine of the mean.

▶ The doctrine of the mean

The doctrine of the mean is based on the insight that in any kind of activity, one can have too much of something, too little of that thing, or just the right amount. For instance, in a healthy diet, one can have too much salt, but also too little. The right amount Aristotle calls 'the mean'.

The term 'mean' is borrowed from mathematics where it describes the average of two or more numbers. For instance, the mean of one and nine is five, as that is the number exactly between the two. However, when applied to human conduct, the mean is not arrived at by 'splitting the difference' in this way. The right amount of salt in one's diet cannot, for example, be discovered by dividing one extreme amount with one deficient amount. Judgement is required to determine the mean, not crude mathematics.

Virtues also need to be understood in relation to the doctrine of the mean. We are used to thinking of virtues as being opposites of vices. So, for instance, generosity is the opposite of meanness, bravery the opposite of cowardice. For Aristotle, however, the virtues are in fact means between two extremes, one of deficiency and one of excess. So generosity is the mean between a deficiency – meanness – and an excess – which we might call prodigality. Bravery is the mean between a deficiency – cowardice – and the excess – rashness.

Again, it needs to be stressed that the mean is not some half-way point between each extreme. In many cases, the mean lies closer to one end than the other. So, for instance, the mean of bravery is probably closer to rashness than it is to cowardice. Aristotle is also practical enough to realise that where the mean lies varies according to circumstances and sometimes even to the individual. What would be brave when the danger is limited, for instance, might be rash when the situation is perilous. What would be generous for someone of moderate wealth might be prodigal for someone who has little.

Aristotle sums up the role of the mean in virtue by saying: 'Virtue is a purposive disposition, lying in a mean that is relative to us and determined by a rational principle, and by that which a prudent man would use to determine it' (1107a). The stress here on 'purposive disposition' and 'rational principle' shows how, for Aristotle, being virtuous is not a matter of luck or innate character, but of cultivating ones character (dispositions) in accordance with rationality. Once again, as in the previous section, we see here the hallmark of Aristotle's thinking about human flourishing requiring a combination of reason and habit.

In the *Ethics*, Aristotle spends a fair amount of time applying the doctrine of the mean to various virtues. It is worth reading these passages, particularly to see how, in applying the principle, Aristotle always tries to fit the theory to the facts and not the other way around.

However, if one really wants to understand the doctrine of the mean, perhaps the best way is to play with the concept yourself. Start by making a list of 'virtues', such as patience, modesty and friendliness. Next, try to think what the excess of each virtue is. (Weakness? Shyness? Obsequiousness?) Then see what the deficiency is. (Impatience? Boastfulness? Unfriendliness?) Then try to judge where the mean falls between the two. Finally, consider how your judgement about where the mean might fall differs according to circumstances. Can you think of two occasions where what would be boastful in one would be modest in the other? For example, on a CV one is expected to list one's good points and achievements. But if one were to do the same thing in casual conversation, one would appear to be very boastful.

Exploring the concept of the mean in this way is, I think, more fruitful and interesting than simply reading Aristotle's catalogue of virtues – though one should do that too!

▶ The role of pleasure

All this talk of happiness and virtue can strike the modern ear as rather puritanical and dull. Where is the place in all this for pleasure? We are used to thinking that the pursuit of pleasure is, if not the highest good, then at the very least an important part of the good life. Virtually every advertisement, for example, sells its product on the basis of the (often pseudo-sexual) pleasure it will give us. To enjoy pleasure seems to be the most natural thing in the world. So where does it come into the Aristotelian good life?

Throughout its history philosophy has tended to be critical of placing too much emphasis on pleasure. Even the supremely hedonistic utilitarian philosophy of J. S. Mill, which considered the highest good to be the maximisation of pleasure and minimisation of pain, managed to none the less dismiss most ordinary pleasures of the flesh as 'lower pleasures', inferior to the higher pleasures of the intellect.

If the great philosophers have all been united in their distrust of pleasure, perhaps we should take this to be a sign that we, too, ought to be suspicious of its allure. Aristotle is an excellent guide here because, unlike Plato for instance, he does not seem to be pathologically averse to pleasure, he simply thinks it needs to be in its proper place.

One reason why we have to not just give in to pleasures is simple: 'Pleasure induces us to behave badly, and pain to shrink from fine actions' (1104b). A little reflection surely confirms that this is true. Although most of the time it is harmless or even beneficial to indulge our pleasures, when we do act wrongly, more often than not we do so because we were tempted by the promise of pleasure. We don't need to restrict ourselves to the repeated instances of sexual infidelity to provide examples. People steal because they want to enjoy the pleasures the stolen object can give them. People lie in order to obtain rewards that would otherwise elude them.

Similarly, we often avoid doing the right thing because it is too painful. We lie rather than confront an unpleasant truth. We allow people to suffer because we can't be bothered to endure the inconvenience helping out would require.

Aristotle's point is not that pleasure inevitably leads to harm or that it is only by enduring pain that we do good. It is rather that if we allow ourselves to be controlled by our desire for pleasure and our aversion to pain, then inevitably, from time to time we will be unable to stop ourselves doing the wrong thing.

The solution to this is not to avoid pleasure and pain, but to be in control of our relationship to them. We need to be able to have the discipline and self-control to be able to decide when to indulge our pleasures and when to refrain, when to shirk from pain and when to confront it.

Further, our moral character will actually determine what we see as painful or pleasant. Someone who has cultivated a virtuous character will, for example, find doing the right thing pleasurable and the wrong thing irksome. They will be able to resist the temptation of acts which are initially pleasant but ultimately bad for us and they will be able to endure with equanimity the pains involved in doing the right thing when it is difficult to do so.

We can see, then, that Aristotle is no knee-jerk opponent of pleasure. Pleasure does play a part in the good life. What Aristotle stresses is that the way we mould our character also moulds our attitude to pleasure and pain, both by putting us, rather than them, in control and by changing the very things we find pleasant or painful.

Aristotle also has some interesting things to say about the nature of pleasure itself. His own view contrasts markedly with that of Plato. Plato argued that pleasure and pain were both processes (see the dialogue *Philebus*). The way he saw it, the healthy individual is in a state of equilibrium, with no pain and no pleasure. He saw both pain and pleasure as arising out of a disruption of this equilibrium. For example, when a healthy individual (no pleasure or pain) becomes ill, their equilibrium is disrupted and this results in their feelings of pain. As they recover, they feel pleasure. Things that are normally neutral, such as walking about, feel pleasurable because the person is returning to equilibrium.

A similar process can occur in the opposite direction. When a person gets drunk, they disrupt their equilibrium and for a while feel very pleasant. But the body needs to return to its usual balanced state and, when it does so, there are corresponding feelings of pain, manifest in this instance in headaches, vomiting or other hangover symptoms.

On this view, it seems pleasure is not worth having because pleasure cannot be separated from pain: one only feels pleasure if one is in a process which involves at least an equal amount of pain.

Aristotle does not object to this account directly, but his view that pleasure is not a process does run counter to that of Plato. He believes that pleasure does not have the distinctive features of processes, which are characterised by being activities over time which are complete when an end is achieved (1174b). The process of building, for example, takes place over many days and concludes when the given construction is complete. Pleasure is just not like this at all. Pleasure is a feeling and at any given moment it is complete in itself. It is not something which is felt to achieve some end: it is an end in itself.

Clearly, this account contradicts that of Plato and, here, experience seems to support Aristotle. Although it is true that some pleasures are the flip sides of corresponding pains, many are not. We do not pay for the pleasure of enjoying a good film with pain afterwards, for instance. Rather than viewing pleasure in this way, Aristotle sees it as occurring whenever a particular faculty is in good condition and is directed towards its proper object (1174b). For example, when the eye is in good condition and it is directed at what is truly beautiful, we enjoy the most perfect pleasures of sight. Our highest pleasure, therefore, is when our highest faculty – the intellect – is in good working order and is considering intellectual matters.

In both these examples, as for all pleasures, there is an activity which is productive of pleasure. But to say pleasure is an activity is not to say it is a process. For example, dancing is an activity, but it is not a process because it does not have as its goal some end-product or result: it is enjoyed for its own sake. In the same way, pleasure too is an activity but is not directed at any goal, except in the sense that to enjoy proper pleasures is part of living the good life and thus achieving the proper end or goal for humankind.

Pleasure is, then, part of the good life. Indeed, Aristotle acknowledges it is essential (1175a). But pleasure needs to be understood properly. The pleasure a bad person gets from harming someone is in a sense not a genuine pleasure at all, since it is not the pleasure that is achieved by a person exercising their faculties according to their proper function. The virtuous person enjoys pleasures, but they are the calm pleasures of a person in control and at ease, not the frantic pleasures of someone lunging from one experience to the next.

We saw earlier that the good life involves happiness, self-sufficiency and is lived in accordance with our proper function as rational beings. We have spent some time looking at happiness and pleasure as well as at one rational principle – the doctrine of the mean. We need now to turn to the other rational principles that govern the good life.

▶ Choice, freedom and responsibility

If we are to lead a life governed by reason, then that means being able to make choices on the basis of our own rational deliberations. Because of this, the idea that we live in accordance with our nature as free, rational beings is central to Aristotle's conception of the good life. But what does it mean to act freely?

Aristotle answers this question by distinguishing between acts which are voluntary and those that are not. In this latter class he talks of several varieties of act: the involuntary, the non-voluntary and the compulsory (1110a). We need to consider each one.

Compulsory acts are those to which the agent (the person acting) contributes nothing at all and are a sub-species of involuntary acts – acts that occur against our will. If, for example, you were driving your car and it were blown off the road by high winds, then the act of driving the car off the road would have been compulsory. But if I am forced to pull up because of the high winds, then the act is not compulsory – since I contribute something to it. Nevertheless, it is involuntary because I didn't want to pull up at that time and was in a sense forced to do so.

It is clear that very few acts are truly compulsory and in fact, when they are compulsory in this sense, we tend to talk not about acts of agents, but of things that happen to agents. Many more acts are involuntary but not compulsory.

However, it is not easy to decide whether many particular acts are genuinely involuntary in this weaker sense. This is another area where the subject matter allows for only a small degree of precision. For example, if I have to throw objects out of a hot air balloon to stay afloat, on the one hand it seems I was forced to do it, and so the act is involuntary; but on the other, I could have done otherwise and crashed – it was my choice which stopped me doing so. So there is a grey area between voluntary and involuntary acts. Here, we need to talk about degrees of compulsion rather than talking about the act being involuntary *or* voluntary.

There is another species of involuntary act and that is one which is performed out of ignorance. This ignorance can be about one of five things: the act itself, the object of the act, the instrument of the act, the aim of the act or the manner of the act. Take, for example, a case of involuntary killing, let's say an 'accidental' shooting of a person. One might be ignorant of the act, because one doesn't know that firing a pistol aimed at someone means that the person gets shot. One could be ignorant of the object of the act, because one might not know that the person one is shooting is in fact that person (or a person at all). One might be ignorant of the instrument of the act because one doesn't know that what one is holding is a gun, rather than a toy or replica. One might be ignorant of the aim of the act because one might think that it is required to shoot the person to save them, or others, from death. And one might be ignorant of the manner of the act since one only intended to injure rather than kill the other person.

In all these cases a form of ignorance meant that the act of killing was involuntary – it was not what the agent intended to do.

Aristotle also introduces a further category, that of the non-voluntary act. This is when someone acts through ignorance, in any of the ways described above, but feels no subsequent pain or remorse. It is not clear whether Aristotle intends this to cover people who never discover their ignorance, people who discover their ignorance but are not bothered by it, or both. Nor is it really clear why we need this category at all. Aristotle simply says that since there is a difference between the person who feels pain and remorse because of their ignorance and the person who doesn't, it is best to have a way of distinguishing between them.

This cataloguing of the various forms of involuntary action allows Aristotle to come up with a clearer conception of a voluntary act. A voluntary act, Aristotle says, 'would seem to be one of which the originating cause lies in the agent himself, and who knows the particular circumstances of his action' (1111a). In other words, it is an act free of compulsion and ignorance.

Though this may seem uncontroversial, we have reason to be suspicious of the idea of an act originating in ourselves. We are in many ways the products of our social environment and our genes. The cause of an act never, it seems, stops with me, in some faculty called the 'will'. Rather, if I choose to do this or that, it always seems possible to explain why I made the decision in a way which brings in causes external to me (such as my genetic make up or my environment). Aristotle's account of free will is therefore open to attack.

Developing his account further, Aristotle argues that only some voluntary acts are truly chosen. Some acts are voluntary, in that they originate from us and are not made in ignorance, but they arise out of desire, temperament or opinion. Aristotle wants to say that as these are not rooted in rational principles, they are not genuine choices. Choice is that kind of voluntary act which is made after deliberation.

Deliberation (*bouleusis*) is a particular kind of reasoning. It is not reasoning about eternal truths, nor is it reasoning about what ends are worth pursuing. Rather, deliberation is reasoning about the means to an end. When one deliberates one thinks about what is in one's power to do and what action can best bring about the right end. We will look at the different kinds of reasoning in the next two sections.

The ideas of choice and freedom are naturally related to those of responsibility, praise and punishment. Aristotle maintains that only those acts that are voluntary merit praise, blame or punishment (1113b). However, Aristotle is also quite conservative on this matter and does not countenance the possibility that some people might be bad involuntarily. In his subsequent discussion he deals with several examples of where someone might appear to be acting involuntarily, but Aristotle still thinks blame is suitable.

One easy example is the case of someone who does wrong when drunk. The person may not have known what they were doing, and in that sense were ignorant and therefore acting involuntarily. But they made the initial choice to get drunk and so they must ultimately be responsible for their actions.

However, Aristotle extends this kind of reasoning to less plausible examples. In any case, it seems, when a person has a bad moral character and this leads them to act badly, perhaps in ignorance of what is good, he claims that there was a time when the person in question could have chosen to go down a different road. 'It was at first open to the unjust and licentious persons not to become such, and therefore they are voluntarily what they are', he argues. This stress on the ultimate responsibility of the individual for their moral character may seem naïve to modern readers. When we read about the lives, for example, of young people from disadvantaged backgrounds whose lives start on a spiral of crime at a very young age, we often get the feeling that the delinquency was in some way inevitable. It seems harsh to say that this person could have just chosen to live a good, upright life. They were surrounded by crime, not given a safe home to live in and made to feel bad about themselves. In the face of this, Aristotle's faith in people's ability to make of themselves what they will seems idealistic.

▶ Five routes to truth

Aristotle stresses the role of rationality in the good life and the *Ethics* contains a detailed account of the different types of 'intellectual virtue', or types of reasoning.

Aristotle starts by making a distinction between two types of intellect: the contemplative and the calculative (1138b). Contemplative reason is concerned with the discovery of first principles, or truths which are fixed and invariable. Calculative intellect (or deliberation, see the section on choice, freedom and responsibility), in contrast, is concerned with what is changeable or variable. For example, thinking about the nature of justice is a job for the contemplative intellect, but making decisions about how to implement justice in a particular instance is a function of calculative intellect.

Philosophers are usually thought of as people who are so caught up in contemplative reasoning that they are fairly impractical people and thus poor at calculative reasoning. Aristotle's distinction explains how this can be so while reminding us that both types of intellect are important and both are needed if we are to live our lives fully, according to our function as rational beings. We need both to be able to identify what is true and good absolutely (using contemplative reasoning) and to be able to order our actions and desires so that we are led towards the Good in our everyday lives (using calculative reasoning).

Having made this basic distinction, Aristotle goes on to catalogue the different 'modes of thought' or ways of reasoning to reach truth (1139b). Here, I shall simply go through them one by one.

Scientific knowledge or *epistēmē* is perhaps misleadingly named, since Aristotle characterises it as being that branch of knowledge which is concerned with what is necessarily true, true eternally. It works by making inferences from first principles which are fixed and certain, though our reasoning from them may be subject to error.

At first this seems puzzling since we are used to thinking of science as something which is much more in flux – theories come and go and are improved on or rejected by subsequent generations. Philosophically speaking, we often contrast the uncertain nature of scientific knowledge with the fixed certainties of mathematics and logic.

In one way, we need not worry about this anomaly, since all translations are approximate and words change their usage, so we should not expect what Aristotle meant by 'science' to correspond exactly to what we mean by it. But there is also a more instructive way of solving the puzzle, by thinking our way back to Aristotle's time and considering what it would be reasonable to accept as eternal, certain first principles. What we need to realise is that the sharp distinction between empirical subjects, where experience is the guide, and *a priori* subjects, where the intellect alone reigns, had not yet been made. Many of what we would now consider to be empirical hypotheses were considered to be *a priori* true. For instance, we have seen how Aristotle reasoned that everything has its proper function (*telos*) and how one needs to understand this *telos* in order to understand its essence (see the section on teleology) This, for Aristotle, would constitute one of the first principles which form the foundations of *epistēmē*. Seen this way, it is not so surprising that some science appeared to belong to the realm of that which was fixed and certain.

If *epistēmē* makes inferences from first principles, how are these first principles themselves known? They cannot themselves be demonstrated by *epistēmē*, since *epistēmē* itself makes its demonstrations from first principles. Therefore, the truth of first principles must in some way be directly apprehended. We do this with the faculty of *nous* or intuition.

This species of knowledge is problematic for philosophy. There always has to be a point where rational reflection ceases, a point where we can longer provide arguments but simply have to accept that something is just true. In later philosophy, these truths have typically been restricted to those which are self-evident, or those which cannot be denied without contradiction. Aristotle's conception of *nous* puts a name to the faculty which recognises these truths which cannot themselves be demonstrated, but in the *Ethics* he gives no account of how we are to recognise whether we are using this faculty correctly.

We can see how *epistēmē* and *nous* complement each other. When a person has mastery of both – when they can grasp first principles and reason properly from them – we say that this person has wisdom or *sophia*.

Art or technical skill – *technē* – is a productive form of intelligence and is concerned with such things as building, carving or constructing. The important thing to note here is that to truly qualify as *technē* the production must be properly reasoned. For example, a well-designed suspension bridge is an excellent example of *technē*, while my feeble attempts at putting up some wonky shelves most certainly is not.

Phronēsis is usually translated as prudence or practical wisdom. It is a species of calculative intellect for it is not concerned with determining what the good is, but with how best to live in order to attain that good. In everyday parlance one could describe this as common sense: the ability to make the right choices on a day to day basis which enables one to live a good life.

The political sciences are a form of prudence, but a prudence concerned with the state rather than the individual. In the forming of legislation and in the day to day work of politics, one needs this kind of good judgement about what will produce the best results. This practical, applied knowledge, however, differs from *sophia*, in that it is informed by, and concerned with, the changing actual world around us rather than eternal truths.

Epistēmē, nous, sophia, phronēsis and *technē* are the five forms of intellect which are considered most important. But there are others. *Euboulia* is glossed as resourcefulness, though this is not a particularly illuminating translation. It is a type of good deliberation, and as we have seen, deliberation is thinking about the means to ends, not about ends themselves. Good deliberation means not only thinking properly, but thinking properly about the right end: working out the best way to do harm, for example, is not an example of *euboulia*.

Understanding or *sunesis* is best understood in contrast with *phronēsis*. While both are concerned with everyday life, rather than eternal truths, they are different in that *phronēsis* is concerned with determining the right action while *sunesis* is simply about understanding. For example, a person who can understand why the situation in the Middle East is as it is demonstrates *sunesis*. But only if they are able to come up with some kind of plan of action to make things better can they be said to have *phronēsis*.

Aristotle has little to say about judgement or *gnōmē* except that it is the virtue which allows people to make equitable or fair decisions. A good judge in a court of law needs to be able to demonstrate *gnōmē* .

A final intellectual faculty is cleverness or *deinotēs*, which is the ability to carry out actions so as to achieve a goal. This differs from the others we have considered in that it can be used for good or for bad. We can talk about a diabolic plot being clever if the agent used ingenious means to do harm, just as we can talk about a clever solution to a genuine problem.

The intellectual virtues have two kinds of value: intrinsic and extrinsic. To say they are intrinsically valuable is to say that they are valuable in themselves. In Aristotle's view, exercising our intellectual faculties in accordance with our nature is good regardless of what other benefits they help us to accrue. But they are also extrinsically valuable in that they help us to achieve the highest good, which is happiness.

The intellectual virtues also complement one another. One's intellect is in a sense more complete if one is able to demonstrate several of the virtues rather than just one or two. Obviously, people can be stronger in some than others, but one should never neglect entirely one at the expense of another if one wants to have a well-rounded intellect.

▶ Conclusion

The *Ethics* is very much a work of practical benefit. Unlike much philosophy, it is both an enquiry into truth and a kind of handbook for living well. For this reason, there are several 'take home' messages from it.

Aristotle provides three rules for good conduct (1109b). He advises we avoid extremes in order to increase our chances of hitting the mean. We need to be alert to our own errors so we can correct our faulty inclinations and pull ourselves back towards the right path. And we need to make sure that we are not slaves to pleasure and pain, but always be careful that they do not lead us astray.

Aristotle ends the *Ethics* by warning that all we have learned in it will be useless unless we can put it into practice (1179b). To do this we need to be able to start with a decent character. This is why Aristotle stresses that the formation of good character is the most important thing in education. A person of bad character just won't be receptive to the lessons he has to teach us.

Aristotle thinks that the state has the most important role to play here as it has an authority a parent lacks. With our experience of the terrible things a too-powerful state can do, we may be less optimistic here than Aristotle. Remember that he would have been thinking about reasonably small city-states, not the much larger countries most of us now live in. He does think that, in the absence of a strong state lead, parents can do the job, but he advises that to do so they need to understand and act rather like legislators themselves. Again, this might sound naïve to modern ears: we know too well that when parents adopt rigid 'systems' to bring up their children, the results are often inferior to upbringings based on more common-sense notions of providing love, security and clear boundaries for behaviour.

Who is to provide a lead in all of this? Although Aristotle does not go so far as Plato and propose that our rulers are philosopher-kings, he clearly does believe that we can only bring this to fruition if we apply ourselves to what he calls politics – the strand of philosophy which has been the subject matter of much of the *Ethics*. Given the remarkable breadth of Aristotle's *Ethics* and the way in which it touches on so many different branches of knowledge, perhaps this is a fair conclusion. For when Aristotle says we must be led by philosophy, he is not talking about a narrow, abstract discipline, but a wonderfully rich and diverse subject which has perhaps never been explored with as much insight as in the *Ethics*.

Summary

Aristotle's *Ethics* is about the way we ought to live. It is both an enquiry into truth and a kind of handbook for good living. Aristotle argues that it is worth nothing if it is not put into practice.

At the root of his investigation is his **teleology** – the view that one best understands what something is by looking at what goal or end it is directed towards. In the case of humans, our end is called **the Good**. Aristotle argues that this end is a kind of self-sufficient happiness, for happiness is the one thing that is valued solely as an end, not as a means.

Happiness is reached when we live according to our proper function as rational beings. Happiness is not to be confused with pleasure or public honour. Although pleasure has a role to play in the good life, we need always to be in control of pleasure (and pain) rather than allow pleasure to be our master. Because pleasure is something animals also enjoy, it cannot be our highest good since it is not a part of humanity's distinctive essence.

Happiness is not a state but a kind of activity, which again explains how it is reached by us performing our proper function. **Contemplation** plays an important part in this since in contemplation we are exercising our highest faculty, that which differentiates us from animals.

Moral **virtue** is 'a purposive disposition lying in a **mean**'. It is purposive because we cannot be accidentally good – being good requires acting freely, in knowledge of what the Good is, in order to do that good. It is a disposition because we can only be good if we cultivate our characters so that we are habitually good. It lies in a mean because the right action is always the correct balance between two extremes.

Our actions can be **voluntary**, involuntary or non-voluntary, and only actions which are voluntary merit praise, blame, reward or punishment. However, when we act in ignorance and are responsible for that ignorance, we cannot avoid responsibility.

The intellect is divided between the **contemplative** and the **calculative**. There are five main intellectual virtues: scientific knowledge (***epistēmē***), intuition (***nous***), wisdom (***sophia***), art or technical skill (***technē***) *and* prudence or practical wisdom (***phronēsis***).

Glossary

Calculative intellect   The part of the intellect that is concerned with achieving ends, rather than determining what the right ends are.

Contemplation   The highest of humanity's faculties, since it is what distinguishes us from animals.

Contemplative intellect   The part of the intellect that is concerned with reasoning about ultimate ends rather than the means to them.

Deinotēs   Cleverness, which can be used for good or bad purposes.

Epistēmē   Knowledge gained by sound reasoning from first principles, which are themselves certain.

Euboulia   Good deliberation, which enables us to achieve appropriate ends.

Eudaimonia   Happiness or human flourishing. The highest good of humankind.

Gnōmē   Good judgement to determine what is fair.

The Good   The ultimate end or goal for humankind.

The mean   The point between two extremes where moral virtue is found.

Nous   A form of intuition which enables us to know the first principles from which all sound reasoning proceeds.

Phronēsis   The practical wisdom to understand what needs to be done in a given situation to achieve a good result.

Sophia   Wisdom, which is achieved when *epistēmē* and *nous* work together.

Soul   Not a kind of spiritual entity, but the way in which the parts of an individual work together as a whole.

Sunesis   Understanding which does not necessarily result in the knowledge of what the best action is.

Technē   Art or technical skill, practised according to rational principles.

Teleology   The view that one best understands something's essential nature by finding out what its distinctive goal or function is.

Virtue   The operation of any faculty, moral or intellectual, in accordance with its true function.

Voluntary   An act is voluntary when its originating cause lies within the agent performing the act, who knows the particular circumstances of his action.

Further reading

Many editions of the *Ethics* are available. I would recommend J. A. K. Thomson's translation (Penguin Classics) for its clarity and its helpful layout. All quotes in this chapter come from this edition. The *Metaphysics* is probably the work by Aristotle one should read next.

Aristotle on Ethics by Gerard J. Hughes is another excellent volume in the Routledge GuideBook series. It provides a systematic and thorough overview of Aristotle's moral thought.

Jonathan Barnes's *Aristotle* remains the best introduction to the philosopher's thought in general and it is now available as part of Oxford University Press's excellent series of *Very Short Introductions*.

Another good short introduction is *Aristotle* by Kenneth McLeish, part of the *Great Philosophers* series published by Phoenix. The book also appears as part of the anthology of the series, the *Great Philosophers*, edited by Ray Monk and Fredric Raphael (Vintage).

2 René Descartes: *Meditations on First Philosophy* (1641)

▶ Background

Descartes's *Meditations* is one of the most important works in the rationalist tradition of philosophy. Rationalism is characterised by a belief that all the major problems of philosophy – and perhaps all the major intellectual problems of the world, full stop – can be answered by the application of rational thought alone.

Rationalists believe that one can understand the fundamental nature of reality just by thinking clearly about it and reasoning from 'first principles': self-evident truths that no-one can deny. This reasoning will be deductive in nature. That is to say, arguments will proceed from premises to conclusions by a logic-ally water-tight method. In this way, arguments in philosophy are like sums in mathematics. Just as we add together two numbers to produce a third, so we can add together two propositions (premises), such as 'Lions are mammals' and 'Mammals do not lay eggs' to produce a third proposition (conclusion): 'Lions do not lay eggs'. This method of reasoning is as secure as maths and if we follow it, we can achieve the same degree of certainty in philosophy as we do in arithmetic and geometry.

As we shall see when we look at Hume's *Enquiry concerning Human Under-standing*, there are grave difficulties with this rationalist approach. But its attrac-tions should be obvious. For example, many people, from the comfort of their armchairs, consider questions such as the nature of time and wonder if time could have an end. This seems crazy, for if time ended, then there would be something which came after time. But if there is an after-time, then time hasn't ended at all, since the whole notion of 'after' is a temporal one. Therefore, time has no end.

Whenever someone reasons like this, they are reasoning in the spirit of rationalism. However, though such arguments can seem convincing, in the light of contemporary physics we have good reasons not to trust them. The argu-ment about time offered above, for example, is far too simplistic and naïve, despite its intuitive plausibility. It is based on the common-sense idea that there must always be something which comes after something that has ended.

But this common sense is contradicted by Einstein's theory of relativity, which argues that the idea of 'after time' makes no sense, since 'after' is itself a temporal notion. The question 'What comes after time?' is therefore meaningless.

The *Meditations* is one of the paradigms of rationalism and its success or failure to a certain degree reflects the success or failure of rationalism. This is what makes it such an interesting text to read, despite the fact that so much of what it argues appears to be hopelessly wrong! But we should also be careful not to dismiss the *Meditations* so easily. It is a remarkably rich text and if one returns to it, one always discovers something new to take away. It is too easy to dismiss it as obviously wrong, for even where Descartes does go astray, his errors are highly instructive and go to the heart of many fundamental issues in the methodology and principles of philosophy.

▶ The text

The *Meditations* is written as if it were a diary written over six consecutive days. This is modelled on the religious retreat, where people would enter a monastery or similar institution for seven days to pray and contemplate. As with the creation myth of *Genesis*, there are six days of work – the meditations themselves – while the seventh day is one of rest.

Of course, the impression that the book was written over six consecutive days is a literary device. One reason for writing the book in this way is that it gives the reader a framework within which to read it. One could, and perhaps should, read the *Meditations* over six nights, making sure than one allows plenty of time to think about the contents of each meditation before moving on to the other. The model of the retreat thus provides a model for the reader, who is encouraged to approach the text with unhurried contemplation.

There are also pragmatic reasons why Descartes might have wanted the structure of the book to echo that of a religious retreat. Many saw his rationalist approach to questions of God's existence and the nature of the soul as heretical and, indeed, the *Meditations* was banned by the Catholic Church for many years. By presenting the book in an essentially religious mode, Descartes perhaps hoped to reassure the religious authorities of its piety.

Descartes took the unusual step of inviting objections to his arguments from eminent colleagues and publishing these, along with his replies, in the book. (The Cambridge University Press edition of the book contains a helpful selection of these.) This reinforces the sense that this is a text for the reader to grapple and argue with for themselves. It is not a treatise to be digested and regurgitated but an argument in which the reader must participate. The book should be read in this spirit.

▶ First meditation

Descartes starts the *Meditations* with an explanation of what motivated him to write it. He believed that 'it was necessary . . . to demolish everything completely and start again right from the foundations if I wanted to establish anything at all in the sciences that was stable and likely to last.' To reach certain knowledge, it is necessary to eliminate all beliefs that could be doubted and keep only those of which he could be certain. In the objections and replies, he offers a metaphor to explain this idea. If there are some rotten apples in your basket, the best way to eliminate them is to tip out the basket, examine each apple one by one, and only place back into the basket those that are definitely good. Similarly, Descartes will reject all his beliefs, and only accept anew those which prove to be certain. Hence, doubting everything is a *method* of reaching certain truth, a means to an end, not an end in itself. This is an important point to remember, since many casual readers believe Descartes's purpose is to make us more doubtful, rather than to simply use doubt to make us more certain.

Descartes also notes that it is not necessary to consider each of his beliefs one by one if he is to doubt them: 'Once the foundations of a building are undermined, anything built on them collapses of its own accord.' To cast doubt on his beliefs he need only consider the foundations of his beliefs.

Aiming to get at the root of his beliefs, Descartes first considers his senses, which he believes are the source of many of his beliefs. On reflection, it does seem that most, if not all, of our ideas have their origin in what we see, hear, taste, touch or feel. Descartes's argument that all beliefs based on the senses should be considered uncertain can be summarised as:

'From time to time I have found that the senses deceive.'
'It is prudent never to trust completely those who have deceived us even once.'
Therefore, it is prudent not to trust our senses completely.

Although this argument appears sound, the conclusion, as it stands, does not justify wholesale doubt. As Descartes puts it, surely only madmen can doubt all everyday sense-based beliefs. All his argument means is that we should not *completely* trust our senses.

However, so long as there is doubt that some of our sense-based beliefs are false and there is no way of telling which of our sense-based beliefs are true and which are false, we are unable to completely trust any particular sense-based belief. It is as though you have 100 coins and know that one is a fake, but not which one. This means that when you pick any coin, you cannot be sure it is genuine. Similarly, once the seed of doubt is sewn, all beliefs become uncertain.

Descartes also confronts the madman objection more directly by claiming that we cannot be sure we are not like madmen ourselves. His argument goes something like this:

> When I sleep, I have sense experiences of things which do not exist.
> 'There are never any sure means by means of which we can distinguish being awake from being asleep.'
> Therefore, there is no sure means of knowing whether the things I experience through my senses exist or not.

If this is true, then we could be like madmen in that all we take to be true could be illusory, a mere dream. Descartes accepts this argument. Without any way of being sure if we are asleep or awake, there is room for us to doubt that we are awake and hence room for us to suspect that all our waking experience is a lie.

As you will have noticed, the first meditation, like much of the rest of the book, is proceeding like an argument or debate, with Descartes playing the role of both critic and defender. For every argument he puts forward, he considers an objection and then either accepts it or offers a reply. This reinforces the sense of the *Meditations* as a practical course of argument which the reader should engage in.

Continuing with the argument, Descartes considers an objection which suggests his dreaming argument does not justify wholesale doubt. Though it is true that all the particular things we perceive may not exist, there must exist some general types of things from which our illusions are fashioned. Compare this to a painting of, say, a dragon. Of course, dragons may not exist, but all the elements – heads, eyes, tails, fire and so on – do exist. If they did not, then we would be unable to imagine a creature comprising them all.

But then doubt comes back. Surely any composite thing could be invented. Even an eye can be imagined from the basic raw materials of shape and colour. In our dreams we can imagine almost anything.

However, even when dreaming some things cannot be doubted, such as the basic concepts of arithmetic and geometry: shape and number. The truths of maths and geometry cannot be doubted because they do not depend on whether things really exist or not. Awake or dreaming, $2 + 2 = 4$ must be true.

At this point Descartes introduces the biggest doubt of them all. It is not beyond God's power to make us believe that something is self-evident even if it is false. God could be deceiving us. Nothing could seem more obvious than the fact that $2 + 2 = 4$, but it is within God's power to make the false look obviously true, so we cannot even be sure that we are right about this.

This raises a problem for the very idea of God himself, which can be stated as:

If God were good, he wouldn't allow me to be deceived.
I am sometimes deceived. (By my senses – see earlier.)
Therefore, God is either not good or doesn't exist.

Descartes clearly isn't convinced by this argument and in the sixth meditation he explains why God allows us to be deceived even though he is good. All he is doing here is considering the ultimate – for him – doubt, that God doesn't exist. If this is the case, he believes that there is even more reason to doubt everything, because that means his own existence must have been a result of chance, which is an imperfect cause more likely to lead to imperfections in his intellect.

For some reason, perhaps so as not to appear blasphemous, instead of considering the possibility that God is a deceiver, Descartes introduces the idea of an evil demon which could be deceiving him into thinking falsehoods even about maths and geometry. The specific form of this device is unimportant. We can think of many reasons why a person may believe falsehoods to be definitely true, such as dreaming, drugs, hypnosis or brainwashing.

Descartes ends the first meditation without any firm knowledge at all. Once he allows that anything he can doubt must be rejected as uncertain and therefore not known, it seems nothing can be known at all. Although Descartes takes us through a structured series of doubts, we could arrive at the same conclusion any number of ways. If we ask the question, 'Is there anything so clear and obvious that it cannot be doubted to be true?', the answer is bound to be, 'no,' with one exception, which we will come to in the second meditation. Hence, the idea of a deceiving demon is perhaps unneccesary.

▶ Problems

Having shown that virtually everything can be doubted and is therefore somewhat uncertain, where do we go from here? Descartes moves on to find out the one fact which cannot be doubted and builds up from there. But perhaps the moral of the story should be that if we say that immunity from doubt is required for something to be true or known, then nothing can be true or known. Therefore, maybe we simply have the wrong idea of what it means to know something. Immunity from doubt is simply too strict a requirement for knowledge.

There are other problems caused by the stress Descartes places on truths which are beyond all doubt. Descartes hopes to build foundations which are true, upon which he can build up truth to an all-encompassing system. But how will he know when he has discovered foundations which are true? He will know because these foundations will be indubitable – above all doubt. Although indubitable does not mean the same as true, Descartes does seem to believe that if X is indubitable, then it is true. (Which is not to say if it is dubitable then it is false.) Is this claim credible?

There are difficulties with this approach. To say X is indubitable is to state a psychological fact: certainty and doubt are states of mind in the person who is certain or doubting. To say X is true or that one knows that X, on the other hand, is to state an *epistemological* truth – something about what is actually known or true. Why should we believe that we can move so easily from psychological facts to epistemological ones? This point is put well in the objections. It seems that nothing is so absurd or irrational that someone either asleep or mad could not believe it to be certain and indubitable.

It doesn't seem contradictory to doubt something we know, or be certain of something that turns out to be false. However, there is a long tradition in philosophy of thinking of knowledge as being a particular state of mind. If we question this assumption, then we strike at the *Meditations* at the root. But this invites further questions, particularly what other tests are there for something to be true?

Some critics have objected to Descartes's idea that the senses deceive, on the grounds that the metaphorical nature of this claim is not fully appreciated. Similarly, when we talk about 'illusions', it is not at all clear that sticks appearing bent in water, or tall objects appearing short in the distance are really illusions at all. Rather, in these cases, things appear to us precisely as they should appear, given the nature of the world and our senses. So perhaps it would be more accurate to talk about 'perceptual errors' rather than illusions and deceptions.

This doesn't eliminate the sceptical doubts, however. The fact that we err about the world and that we cannot easily tell when we are erring is enough to introduce the doubt that our errors could be more general. But now it seems that the error is not necessarily one of our senses, but also of our judgement. If it could be shown that our minds as well as our senses make errors of which they are unaware about the external world, then it is more difficult for Descartes to maintain, as he does, that the mind cannot be in error when it clearly and distinctly perceives ideas. And if the mind is to share the blame with the senses for mistakes, then how can certain knowledge come from the mind?

A further difficulty is that Descartes talks about the senses and our judgments as if these things can be easily separated. But is this really possible? For it to be so would require there to be 'raw sense-data' – perceptions before the mind gets to work on them – and then an interpreting mind. But it is not at all clear that there are such things as raw sense data. Another way to think about this is to ask the question, do we really do two things when we experience the world: perceive *and* judge? If you think we do, try and explain what perceiving without judging is, and how we can do it.

Again, this objection intertwines judgement and sense experience in such a way as to make Descartes's claim that judgement is absolutely distinct from sense experience dubious.

A final difficulty, and one which will be echoed later, is that in order to undertake the meditations, Descartes must be able to distinguish truth and falsehood. He claims that he can, since whatever one clearly and distinctly perceives to be true must be true. Clearly, there must be a difference between what *is* clearly and distinctly perceived and what merely *appears to be* clearly and distinctly perceived. But Descartes does not show what this difference is, and it is hard to see how he could do so.

▶ Second meditation

Having ended the first meditation with no beliefs that are beyond doubt, in the second meditation, Descartes attempts to lay down the foundations which will enable him to rebuild his knowledge on a surer basis. He does this by discovering the one thing that cannot be doubted, and that is that 'I am, I exist'.

Most people are familiar with Descartes's more famous 'I think, therefore I am' (*cogito ergo sum*). But that formulation appears in the *Discourse on Method*, not in the *Meditations*. The difference in wording is significant. 'I think, therefore I am' is in the form of an argument: the fact that 'I am' is deduced from the fact that 'I think'. But 'I am, I exist' is not an argument. Rather, it is an incontrovertible intuition. One directly *apprehends* the fact that one exists as soon as one thinks – one doesn't need to *deduce* that one exists from the fact that one thinks.

Not everyone agrees that one is directly aware of one's own existence in this way. David Hume, in his *Treatise of Human Nature*, for example, argued that when he directed his attention to his own thoughts, all he was aware of were the thoughts themselves. He was not aware of the self which had them. Instead of 'I think, therefore I am', perhaps all Descartes was entitled to deduce was 'I think, therefore there is thought going on'.

Let us suppose that Descartes has established that something 'I' exists. What is this 'I'? Descartes has a two-part argument to answer this question. The first can be summarised as:

1 If I can conceive of myself without a property, then that property is not a part of my essential nature.
2 Of all the properties I think I have, such as the having of a body and the thinking of thoughts, only the fact that I think is 'inseparable from me'.
3 Therefore, it is my essential nature to be a thinking thing, no more, and no less.

This he takes to establish that his essence is that of a thinking thing. But what sort of thing is this? The second part of the argument aims to provide the answer:

4 This mind cannot be a body, as I can conceive of myself without a body.
5 However, it is clearly not nothing, so it must be something.
6 Hence, it must be a different sort of thing to corporeal things. It must be a purely mental substance.

This is a startling conclusion. Descartes has argued that he is, in essence, a kind of non-material substance which thinks, but has none of the properties of matter. It is singular and indivisible since consciousness is a single centre of thought and as such cannot be divided. In short, he claims to have proved the existence of the soul.

▶ Problems

Descartes's argument is endlessly fascinating but appears to have several major flaws. One is that he appears to think that if two *concepts* are separable, then that implies the *things* to which the concepts apply are always separable. We can see this in the first premise of the argument above, which is the general principle: 'If I can conceive of a thing without a property, then that property is not a part of its essential nature.' For example, although all the cars I know of are made of metal, metalness is not part of a car's essential nature, as a car which is not made of metal would still be a car. The same appears to be true of mind and body: body cannot be part of the essence of mind, as a mind without a body would still be a mind.

Nevertheless, Descartes draws a dubious conclusion from this. To see why, we have to distinguish between ontological (concerned with being) and conceptual independence or dependence. For example, a husband is ontologically independent from his wife. That is to say, his existence does not depend upon that of his wife. But the *concept* of a husband is dependent upon the concept of a wife. We could not have the concept of a husband if we didn't have a concept of a wife.

Descartes's argument hinges on the claim that because mind is conceptually independent from body, it must also be ontologically independent. This is a very strong claim and is what distinguishes dualism from other theories of the mind. But why should we accept this? For example, the concept of water is arguably independent from the concept of H_2O, but that is not to say we could ever have water that was not H_2O. Similarly, I can imagine myself existing without a body, but that doesn't mean I actually could exist without my body.

This objection is a denial of the first premises in each part of the summary of Descartes's argument above. This illustrates the potential problems of using imagination as a guide to possibility. The fact that we are not aware of anything physical in our essence and so could imagine being non-physical does not prove that we are in fact non-physical in nature. Just as the fact that many are unaware that being H_2O is part of the essence of water, so it may be true that being physical is part of the essence of being a person.

We can push this objection further and ask if it is even possible to have a clear and distinct idea of oneself without a body. If you think about it, imagining oneself without a body tends to be more of a case of imagining oneself invisible, but still basically in space, interacting with objects via various senses and so on. This sounds suspiciously like having a body! The problem with Descartes is that it is not enough to have a vague idea of oneself without a body: unless this idea is clear and distinct, it cannot be taken to be certain and by his own principles, anything uncertain goes the way of the rotten apples.

Another problem is that Descartes's argument appears to blur the distinction between a thing and what it does. If something walks (performs an action), it doesn't mean it is a walk (is an action). So, if something uses its intellect (performs mental tasks), it doesn't mean it is an intellect (is a mental thing). From the fact that I think, the only thing we can conclude is that whatever I am, I have the faculty of thought. But that doesn't prove that the thing which has this faculty is not corporeal (bodily). In other words, Descartes is wrong to infer from the fact that I think to the fact that I am a mental substance. Gilbert Ryle calls this error Descartes's 'category mistake'. Descartes thought that because the mind didn't have the same properties as body, it must be a different sort of thing to body. But there are other explanations. Mind could be a function of body, for example. This is a denial of the fifth premise above: mind is neither a thing nor a nothing, but rather a feature of a thing, probably the brain.

Descartes's view has one very odd consequence. Because he thinks it is our essence to think, it follows that to stop thinking is to cease to exist. But then, how do we explain times when we are not thinking, such as in sleep? There are three possibilities. The first is that we die when we sleep. This is clearly absurd. The second, which Descartes believed, is that we do always think, only we don't always remember that we have. This is implausible. The third is that it is wrong to say that a mind must always be thinking. Rather, a mind must have the capacity to think. In the same way that it is the essence of a knife that it be suitable for cutting with, not that it always will be cutting, so the essence of mind could be that it *can* think, not that it always *is* thinking. But then, if mind is merely something with the capacity to think, why can't a physical object have this capacity? This third option seems to eliminate the need for special mental substances.

A final worry about Descartes's argument is that it doesn't so much provide a positive description of mind as a negative one. We are left with an account of all the things mind is not: not a bodily structure, not air, not a thing which walks and senses, and so on. If we simply list all the things which a mind is not, have we really thereby said what it is?

▶ The piece of wax

Descartes has argued that the only thing he cannot doubt is that he exists, and that he is a thinking thing (*res cogitans*). However, at first sight, there is something that strikes him as odd about this. He seems to have a clear idea of what corporeal objects are like, but no clear idea as to his own nature. But how can his idea of what can be doubted be less clear than his idea of what is certain? To see if this really is the case, he considers a corporeal object, a piece of wax. How does he reach knowledge about the wax's nature?

The first hypothesis he considers is that he knows an object from his sense perceptions of it. Descartes lists all the features of the wax his senses are aware of: its smell, colour, appearance, texture and so on. But then he notes that all these features can change, and yet he is still aware of it as the same piece of wax. This means that it is not the information he gets from his senses which enables him to identify and know the nature of the wax. All the sense information is liable to change, and yet his knowledge that the wax is still there is constant. Therefore, the senses cannot be the source of his knowledge, so he rejects this hypothesis.

The second hypothesis is that imagination is the source of his knowledge of the wax. By imagination Descartes means to mentally represent sense perceptions (e.g. to picture something). Even though the sense-dependent features such as colour, smell and so on of the wax can change, we also have an idea of it as something extended, flexible and changeable. But imagination cannot give us this idea, because the imagination cannot run through all the possible changes the wax may undergo. Our understanding of what would constitute a piece of wax is wider than all those particular examples we can imagine. So this hypothesis, too, is found wanting.

This leads him to his third hypothesis, that the mind is the source of his knowledge. It is our minds which have an idea of what the wax is and which comprehend its true nature, and this knowledge is far superior to that provided by the senses or imagination. So the mind alone is the source of our knowledge about the world. The mind can conceive of what the wax is, and this goes further than either sensing or imagining can.

So, what I literally perceive is not a piece of wax, or a person, for example. What I perceive are merely collections of shapes, colours, smells and sounds. It is only through the mind that these can be understood as the objects which they are, so it is really more true to say that it is the mind which perceives the wax: the senses merely report the sensible qualities of the wax (its 'incidents'), which are not enough to reveal its true nature. Compare this to a camera. A camera merely records colours, it doesn't interpret what these various colours represent. Similarly, our senses merely report sense information: our minds interpret it.

His considerations about the piece of wax persuade Descartes that, in fact, he does know his own mind more perfectly than corporeal things. The mind is primary – it comes before knowledge of material things – because without the mind we could not even recognise material objects and the fact that we perceive at all confirms that we exist. Both these are reasons for saying that the mind is better known than corporeal objects, despite first appearances suggesting the contrary.

Descartes's conclusion is a little puzzling, because although his reflections do indeed seem to confirm that sense perception depends upon his having a mind, it doesn't seem to illuminate the nature of that mind. Certainly, it establishes that he exists and thinks, but it doesn't seem to reveal anything more about his existence. The discussion of the wax does not seem to add to our understanding of what kind of thing we really are.

It is also unclear how our understanding of the wax is truly independent of our awareness of its incidents – its smell, colour, shape and so on. If you take away the 'incidents' of the wax, just what is it that you have a clear understanding of? Do we really have a clear idea of a piece of wax that doesn't involve reference to these incidents? Perhaps this shows how our understanding is not quite as independent of our senses as Descartes believes.

▶ Third meditation

The first four paragraphs of this meditation reveal something interesting about Descartes's idea of clear and distinct perception, summarise the argument so far and explain why an argument proving God's existence and non-deceiving nature is required if the *Meditations* are to progress.

Descartes has been searching for knowledge that is certain and indubitable. In order to search for something, though, you must be able to recognise it when you find it! So Descartes must have been working with an idea or a feeling of what certain knowledge is like. He claims to know that he exists when he thinks. So how can he know this? Because there is a 'clear and distinct perception' of his own existence. This is not sense perception, but more like mental apprehension. Could this having of a clear and distinct perception be what knowing something for certain is? Descartes thinks so and we can follow through his thinking to complete an implicit deduction to this conclusion:

'[A clear and distinct perception] would not be enough to make me certain ... if it could ever turn out that something which I perceived with such clarity and distinctness was false.'

Clear and distinct perception is enough to make me certain
Something clearly and distinctly perceived cannot be false.

This argument is certainly valid, but it is not sound because it is circular. The first premise is true if the conclusion is true, but the conclusion can only be deduced if we accept the first premise. But is the first premise true? Surely it is possible for something to be clear and make me certain of it, and yet be false? At least some people must have thought that nothing could be more obvious than that the world was flat, and yet they were wrong. Things can appear clear and make a person certain, and yet be false.

Descartes now has a problem. He has resolved only to accept those things that are certain. But things clearly and distinctly perceived are not certain. Indeed, he hasn't managed to explain how we can tell the difference between *really* clearly and distinctly perceiving and only *seeming* to do so. So what is certain to be true? Nothing, it seems, except the fact that he exists. It seems that Descartes has led himself down the dark and narrow path to solipsism – the belief that only my own existence is certain.

Descartes himself thinks there is a way out of this dark hole. The obstacle to overcome is that though he clearly and distinctly perceives that he exists, that $2 + 3 = 5$ and so on, he admits that if God were a deceiver, he could be wrong even here. In other words, if God deceives, then even what he clearly and distinctly perceives could be false. So in order to move ahead with absolute certainty, he must discover whether God exists and whether he is a deceiver. It is vital to realise how important this is for Descartes's project.

▶ The existence of God

Descartes now attempts his first proof for the existence of God. His starting point is considerations about ideas (which also include sensations and perceptions) and how many have their source outside of us. For example, when I feel heat from a fire, it is clear that the source of this perception is not something within me and under my control. I feel the heat whether I like it or not.

The problem is that, although many ideas have their source outside of me, I cannot be sure that the ideas I have truly resemble their causes. For example, a person can be made to feel a burning sensation if they are told something hot is going to pushed against their back and an ice cube is then placed there. So we cannot learn anything about the cause of our ideas just by considering the ideas themselves.

None the less, Descartes does go on to construct an argument for the existence of God based on ideas and their causes. He does this by invoking what we might call the causal reality principle: a principle which Descartes believes is evidently true by 'the natural light'. The natural light is an odd phrase in Descartes. It sounds like something mysterious and mystical, but is generally used to refer to things which are so clear and self-evidently true that they cannot be doubted. The causal reality principle is one such truth and it states that 'there must be at least as much reality in the efficient and total cause as in the effect of that cause'. Put more simply: 'Something cannot arise from nothing, and ... what is more perfect ... cannot arise from what is less perfect.'

Descartes's terminology can make things appear more complex than they are. For instance, he talks about the 'efficient' cause, which in Aristotle's terminology is the event which begins the change that produces the effect. But since he also talks about the 'total' cause, the principle is not narrowed by talk of efficient causes after all. He also talks about ideas or things containing 'more reality', but for our purposes we can take this simply to mean that these things are more perfect or more complete.

Of course, these technical distinctions are important in high-level scholarly debate about Descartes. But for the reader new to the *Meditations*, the causal reality principle can be simply understood as the idea that an effect can never be more than its cause: you only get out what you put in.

How do we get from this principle to God? Well, although almost all our ideas are of things which are no greater than we are, we have one idea which is of something far greater than ourselves: God. By God, Descartes means something which is 'infinite, independent, supremely intelligent, supremely powerful and which created both myself and everything else ... which exists'. Such an idea could not possibly have originated in Descartes himself, so it must have originated in something as great as the idea itself: God. Therefore, God must exist.

This argument seems too quick. Yet despite the slow build up, it is all indeed found in one short paragraph of the *Meditations*. To see if it stands up, we need to unpack it carefully, as Descartes himself does in the remainder of the third meditation, anticipating objections to clarify the argument.

The most obvious objection is that you do not need an infinite being to exist to give you the idea of the infinite. We can arrive at the idea of the infinite by merely negating the idea of the finite. For example, we all know what a piece of string with an end is like. All we need to do is to imagine such a piece of string *without* an end and we have the idea of infinity.

Descartes's response to this is rather unsatisfactory. Since, he claims, the idea of the infinite contains 'more reality' than the idea of the finite, it must be prior to the idea of the finite. This response really lays bare the main weakness of the argument. Descartes's response here is really little more than a reaffirmation of the causal reality principle. This principle states that something less perfect can only be caused by something at least as perfect, and therefore the idea of the finite must have as its cause the idea of the infinite and not vice-versa. But what the piece of string objection really says is that the causal reality principle itself is false. It offers a counter-example. It shows us that, in fact, there is no problem at all in seeing how a greater idea can spring from a lesser one. It is no good turning around and saying this can't be true because of the causal reality principle: the whole point of the counter-example is to show that the causal reality principle is false.

This is the problem of the remainder of the meditation. Descartes considered many objections, but they are all dealt with on the assumption that the causal reality principle is true. So, for example, he argues that the idea of God can't be caused by nothing because nothing can be caused by nothing. Similarly, Descartes considers and rejects the possibility that he is the cause of these ideas because he is greater than he thinks. This is an attempt to offer an alternative explanation of how we get the idea of God within the framework of the causal reality principle.

None of these objections get to the root of the problem, perhaps because Descartes is so convinced that the causal reality principle is manifest by the natural light that he thinks it has no need of any further justification. But there are at least two ways of attacking the principle.

The first is to draw upon the distinction between ideas and things. We might accept it is true that something lesser cannot be the cause of something greater. But that may not mean that something lesser cannot create the *idea* of something greater. For example, maybe I cannot produce something which manifests more intelligence than I have. But I can have the idea of something more intelligent than myself. We are not so limited in our ideas that we cannot conceive of many things greater than ourselves. The causal reality principle has some plausibility when it comes to physical causation, but seems less plausible when applied to the creation of ideas.

The second objection is to question the general truth of the principle itself. The main problem is that the principle is evidently not true if taken at face value. For instance, current scientific theory states that everything around us is the effect of a big bang that heralded the beginning of time and space. In many ways, this complex universe with its manifold life forms is greater than the simple explosion of energy that occurred at the big bang. Yet if the causal reality principle were true, we could never have got from the big bang to here.

It is true that most scientists believe that the total sum of energy in the universe must remain constant. In this sense it is true that nothing comes of nothing. But the causal reality principle seems to imply something broader: that the more complex cannot be caused by the less complex; that the less intelligent can never give rise to the more intelligent; that the smaller can never give rise to the larger; and so on. All these specific claims are contradicted by current science.

Interestingly, even the idea that nothing can come from nothing is being challenged by science. Baffling though it may sound, it is believed that the amount of matter in the universe is exactly balanced by the amount of anti-matter.

In other words, subtract anti-matter from matter and you get zero. This means that the big bang could indeed have come out of nothing – as the net amount of matter in the universe is zero!

The argument Descartes offers is therefore on very shaky ground. It is based entirely on a principle which Descartes believes to be self-evidently true, but which, on reflection, seems much less secure. If Descartes requires a proof for the existence of God for his project to succeed, he needs another one. In the fifth meditation he does indeed try once more. But first, he turns to the question of truth and falsity.

▶ Fourth meditation

In the philosophy of religion, a major issue is the so-called problem of evil: why, if God is all-good and all-powerful, does God allow suffering and evil in the world? Attempts to resolve this problem are known as theodicies. In the fourth meditation, Descartes offers a kind of theodicy to answer the problem of evil's kid brother – the problem of error. Here, the problem is, if God is all-good and all-powerful, why does he allow people to be so mistaken about the nature of reality and his existence? If he does this – which surely he does – it seems he is wilfully allowing the truth to be hidden from us. Why would God want to do that?

Descartes is convinced that whatever the explanation, it cannot be because God wants to deceive us, since trickery and deception involve a lack of perfection and this is contrary to God's nature (which, after the third meditation, he claims to perceive clearly and distinctly). We could question why Descartes is so sure that deception is contrary to God's nature, but at the very least, if God is a deceiver then he is very different to how we usually take him to be.

Descartes's first solution to this problem does not entirely satisfy him. He considers the possibility that it is because his rational capacities are not infinite. In his rather odd language, if God is supreme being and his opposite is non-being, then Descartes, as a mortal human, lies somewhere in between.

The reason this answer does not suffice is that error is not simply a matter of *negation:* of the person in error lacking something. It is also a matter of *privation:* their not having something – knowledge – which they could otherwise have been given. To give an analogy, if a person in a wheelchair cannot reach the buttons on an elevator, then we could say this is because they are not tall enough to reach it. There is a negation – something they lack – which explains why they can't reach the buttons. But surely it is more accurate to say that this is a case of privation: they could have reached the buttons if the designer had placed them more sensitively. In the same way, our error seems not solely to be explained in terms of our limits, but also in terms of what our creator has deliberately made it possible for us to not have.

Before giving another, better explanation, Descartes first builds in some caveats. First, it is not surprising if he doesn't fully understand God's ways, for he is not God. Second, although our error may appear to be a fault in the universe, perhaps if we looked at the universe as a whole, we would see it as essential to its perfect workings. This may seem a bit like cheating, as it implies that even if Descartes fails to explain why God allows error, we shouldn't worry. We just need to trust that God knows best. How we respond to this depends on how we approach this part of the *Meditations*. For people who already believe in God, it can serve as a piece of apologetics: that is to say, it gives a rational account of how the idea of God can be reconciled with the doubts reason produces. If this is how we read it, it only has to find a place for faith within a rational framework, not to justify faith by reason. But if we approach the text as non-believers, these caveats will seem only to be fudges.

So how does Descartes finally explain error? He does so by explaining the different roles of the faculty of knowledge and the faculty of will. These are very different. As finite beings, our knowledge is limited. For this we cannot blame God, for finite beings must have finite intellect. In addition to this faculty, God also gave us free will. Unlike knowledge, however, a free will is not something which admits of greater or lesser degrees. You either have free will or you do not. God does not have more free will than humans in the same way as he has more knowledge. Again, we cannot blame God for this, since if he were to give us free will at all, he had to give it to us all or nothing. We should rather be grateful that he gave it to us at all.

But what happens when you combine a finite intellect with an unlimited freedom? What happens is that humans fail to limit their freedom so it corresponds to the scope of their intellect. On occasions where they should refrain from assenting or dissenting because they don't have the knowledge to make a proper judgement, they sometimes assent or dissent anyway and thus fall into error. Hence, the way to avoid error is to refuse to make any judgement unless one perceives that something is clearly and distinctly true.

Error is thus the improper use of our free will to make judgements that go beyond what we know. This implies no criticism of God because in granting us finite intellect and unlimited will, he gave us as much as he could. Rather, it is our fault if we overextend ourselves by making judgements about things we do not have clear knowledge about.

None the less, there is still a problem: couldn't God have built in a few safety mechanisms? For example, could he not have given us a kind of instinct that made us refrain from overextending our will in this way? Could he not have created us so that we were naturally cautious when making judgements about things not clearly and distinctly perceived to be true, rather than making us the way we are – all too prone to make such errors?

Descartes considers these objections and then pulls from out of his sleeve the 'get out of jail free' cards he showed us earlier: maybe in the grand scheme of things it is better this way and I have no right to question God's reasons for making me the way I am. For the religious believer, such explanations may suffice. But for the person who remains to be convinced, this is a disappointing answer to a major problem with Descartes's argument.

▶ Fifth meditation

As we saw in the third meditation, Descartes needs to prove that God exists, and that he is not a deceiver, in order to remove the doubt that he could be wrong even about such truths as those of mathematics. He made one attempt at this in the third meditation and tries again, using a different strategy, here. The type of argument used is known as the ontological argument for God's existence.

Descartes's approach is to consider God's essence and try to show how God's essence necessitates his existence. He claims to be able to do this without presupposing God exists. How is this done? Descartes starts by considering geometric shapes; in particular, a triangle. An essential property of a triangle is that all its internal angles add up to 180 degrees, and this would be true even if no triangles existed. Further, these properties are objective, and therefore in some sense real. I do not invent them, 'I recognise then whether I want to or not.' So, although there may in fact be no triangles in the world, one is none the less able to deduce the essential nature of triangles from the clear idea we have of them. From this example, he draws the general principle that 'The mere fact that I can produce from my thought the idea of something entails that everything which I clearly and distinctly perceive to belong to that thing really does belong to it,' *whether or not that thing actually exists*. In other words, everything has an essence (essential properties), even if that thing doesn't actually exist. The inventor of the paper clip, for example, knew the essence of paper-clips before he or she had actually created one.

The idea of God is just as clear and distinct as that of a triangle. Therefore, it should be equally possible to deduce God's essence, without presupposing that God exists. Whatever is found to be a part of God's essence is as certain a part of his essence as the properties of a triangle are part of a triangle's essence.

So what is God's essence? The properties which cannot be separated from the idea of God are the properties of having all perfections, hence supreme perfection is God's essence. 'Since existence is one of the perfections', the idea that God exists cannot be separated from his essence. Therefore, God must exist. Existence can no more be separated from God's essence as three-sidedness can be separated from a triangle's essence, and both facts can be known with equal *a priori* certainty. Note that God is unique in this sense. Normally, existence is not part of a thing's essence. But if something is supremely perfect, it must exist, for were it not to exist, it would be less perfect than something identical to it, but existing. But then, it cannot be less perfect than anything, or it would not be supremely perfect. Hence, it exists.

We can consider the argument in another way. Descartes says he has 'countless ideas that, though they may not exist outside of me, still cannot be called nothing, and although not invented by me still have their own nature'. A triangle is one example: it may not exist out of his own mind, but it cannot be called nothing, is not invented by him and has its own nature. God is another such idea, which also may not (at least not be presupposed to) exist outside of him, but is not nothing, is not invented by him and has its own true nature. But with God, as his nature is supreme perfection, he must actually exist.

Descartes illustrates his argument with an analogy. Just as the idea of a mountain cannot be separated from the idea of a valley, so the idea of God cannot be separated from the idea of his existence. Put simply, 'I am not free to think of God without existence', as this would be to think of 'a supremely perfect being without a supreme perfection', which is logically impossible. It is not an assumption that God has all perfections – it is simply a fact which follows from the idea of God itself. Once Descartes has found the clear and distinct idea of God, it is as certain as any other clear and distinct idea.

We can summarise Descartes's argument as follows:

Everything that is clearly and distinctly perceived to belong to a thing really does belong to it.
One cannot think of God except as existing (i.e. one clearly and distinctly perceives that existence is part of God's essence).
Therefore, God must exist.

Descartes is convinced this is true and though when his mind is on other things he may lose sight of the force of the argument, all he needs to do is to bring it to mind to see without doubt that it works. Further, since the argument is based on reason and not on the objects of this experience, the conclusion is true whether he is awake or asleep. In this way, the argument bypasses all his sceptical doubts.

▶ Problems

One common type of objection to this argument was first raised by Immanuel Kant. Although the precise form of the objection varies, what they all have in common is the claim that Descartes is not entitled to deduce that God exists merely from his essence, as existence is not one of those things which can be counted as a property or perfection.

Descartes includes existence among the properties of God, claiming it is one of God's perfections. However, if something doesn't exist, surely it doesn't *lack* a perfection or property; rather it has *no* perfections or properties. If I have 100 real coins and 100 imaginary coins, it seems bizarre to say that the real coins have all the properties of the imaginary ones plus the property of existing. It is more accurate to say that the imaginary coins have no properties at all. This is a way of saying that existence is not a 'perfection' or a 'property'.

Descartes responds by just denying this and saying that necessary existence is very much a property of God since it defines what he is. But if existence is a property of God as a perfect being, then it can be attributed to other perfect beings, such as the perfect heffalump. Since the perfect heffalump has as one of its properties perfection, and perfection implies existence, then surely the perfect heffalump must exist. But that would mean, by the same logic, that the perfect everything must exist, which is surely absurd. (However, it should be noted that Plato's theory of the forms seems to imply just this conclusion.)

Descartes's reply would be to say that God is different because he is supremely perfect, whereas the perfect heffalump is only perfect in certain respects. This is why existence is part of God's perfection, but not that of the perfect heffalump. But it seems that the heffalump argument is enough to show that existence is not a perfection at all, so it is irrelevant that God is supremely perfect – existence just hasn't got anything to do with perfection.

A second type of objection owes its origin to Hume (see Chapter 3 on his *Enquiry concerning Human Understanding*.) Descartes's argument is *a priori* – it is not based on facts gleaned from experience, but on first principles of logic. Many philosophers believe that all *a priori* arguments about matters of actual existence are hypothetical: they tell us what must be true *if* certain premises are true. But whether or not the premises are true is either a matter of fact – and therefore they need to be established by observation not logic – or purely logical, and therefore not a matter of fact or existence.

This point is illustrated by an objection raised by Thomas Aquinas to an earlier version of the argument. Aquinas argued that the fact that the concept of existence is inseparably linked to the concept of a supreme being only tells us about the *concept* of God. It does not follow from this that the existence of God is anything actual. One cannot deduce anything about existence from mere concepts.

This objection is supported by close consideration of Descartes's analogy with mountains and valleys, which perhaps doesn't deliver the conclusion Descartes thought it did. The argument about mountains runs something like this:

A mountain without a valley is a (logical) contradiction.
That which is (logically) contradictory cannot exist.
Therefore, a mountain cannot exist without a valley.

However, if you now replace 'mountain' and 'valley' with 'God' and 'existence', this is what you get:

> God without existence is a (logical) contradiction.
> That which is (logically) contradictory cannot exist.
> God without existence cannot exist.

This is true, but it doesn't show that God must exist. It only shows that if God exists, he exists, which is a tautology. This supports the objection that the ontological argument cannot get beyond facts about the concept of God to facts about the real existence of God.

But perhaps the most famous objection to Descartes's particular use of the ontological argument is known as the Cartesian circle. We are sure that what we clearly and distinctly perceive is true only if God exists. But we can be sure that God exists only if we clearly and distinctly perceive this to be true. But what we clearly and distinctly perceive is true only if God exists, and so on. This creates a vicious circle.

Set out more formally, we can see the circle in action:

1 How do I know God exists?
2 Because I clearly and distinctly perceive he exists.
3 How do I know what I clearly and distinctly perceive is true?
4 Because God exists.
1 How do I know God exists?

> . . .

We need to prove God exists to be sure that we are not mistaken even about apparently self-evident truths. But we cannot prove God exists unless we assume apparently self-evident truths are true. If Descartes is to consistently apply his method of doubt, then he has no right to suspend his doubt that even what he clearly and distinctly perceives is true in order to prove God exists.

Descartes does have a reply. He claims that what he doubts is 'knowledge of conclusions *recalled* when we are no longer aware of them', and that he doesn't doubt things he clearly and distinctly perceives *now*, in other words, self-evident truths, at the time he is aware of them. This is certainly not what he appeared to be saying in the first meditation, and one must ask why self-evident truths that you are currently aware of should be made immune from doubt. His justification for this seems to come in the third meditation, but it is not a convincing one.

We should consider one final, brief objection. Descartes's argument hinges on the fact that the idea of God is as clear and distinct as that of a triangle. This is highly doubtful. Two rational people cannot meaningfully disagree about what a triangle is, such is the clarity of the idea of a triangle. The fact that God's nature is a matter of debate shows that it is not so clear and distinct. The idea of God may also differ from that of a triangle, as it may be invented, which the idea of a triangle isn't.

▶ Sixth meditation

Descartes completes his project of reconstructing his beliefs about the world by turning to material objects. Descartes begins his account with some preliminary remarks concerning the difference between imagination and understanding.

Descartes understands what a triangle is, and when he considers a triangle, he usually imagines a triangle at the same time. But this imagination is not required for understanding. For example, he understands what a chiliagon is (a 1000 sided object), but what he imagines when he thinks of a chiliagon does not form part of that understanding. This can be seen from the fact that his mental image of a chiliagon is not distinct from his mental object of a myriagon. It is merely a vague mental picture of a many-sided shape. Imagining, which we can define as 'the mental representation of sense experiences' is thus distinct from understanding, which is 'to comprehend, or grasp an idea intellectually'.

Descartes has already argued that it is his essence to think, and now he has shown that imagination is not a necessary part of this thinking. As he can thus have a clear and distinct idea of himself as a thinking thing without imagination, it therefore follows that the faculty of imagination is not a part of his essence. Descartes then makes a 'probable conjecture' that he has been endowed with the faculty of imagination because his body exists, and that this gives him ideas of corporeal things, which are the subject matter of imagination. In other words, existent bodies are the most likely source of the contents of his imagination.

But Descartes is not satisfied with this probability and seeks out more certainty. His argument draws together many of the threads that have run through the *Meditations* and can be summarised as follows:

1 Material things can be clearly and distinctly understood, and thus it is within God's power to make them exist.
2 My essence is as a purely thinking thing, which does not have extension as one of its properties.
3 The ideas given to me by sense perception and imagination cannot be understood without the idea of extension.
4 My faculty of sense perception is passive (i.e. I cannot control the nature of what it is I perceive).

5 Therefore, there must be some active faculty producing the ideas given to me in sense perception.

6 This faculty must be external to me, because of (2) and (4).

7 The source of my ideas of material things must either (a) 'contain formally everything which is to be found objectively in the ideas' (i.e. it will actually have the properties of material objects) or (b) 'contain eminently whatever is to be found in the ideas' (i.e. it merely causes the ideas without having the properties of the material objects; a virtual reality machine would be one such cause).

8 Nature leads me to believe (a).

9 Nature is God's creation, and if nature is misleading me into believing (a), then God is deceiving me.

10 God is not a deceiver.

11 Therefore the cause of my ideas of material objects is really existing material objects themselves.

This argument has a beautiful elegance and following its elaborate chain of reasoning can be challenging, but it is ultimately rewarding.

▶ Problems

The main problem with this argument is that it relies heavily on the idea that God is not a deceiver. Unless we can prove this (and it is not clear that Descartes has proved anything about the necessary existence of God), then we cannot conclude that we do not live in a virtual reality environment created by a deceiving demon or a mad scientist.

Also, unless it is true that our essence is that of a purely thinking thing, it is not necessary to suppose that our ideas of material things cannot be the product of our own imaginations, although Descartes does seem right to say that there must be some external cause for our ideas of material objects in general, if not in specific cases.

So to sum up, this is an elegantly constructed, probably valid argument. Its weak links are premise (2), which rests on the arguments of the second meditation, and premises (9) and (10), which rest on the arguments of the fifth meditation. The most telling criticisms of this argument therefore do not concern its structure and presentation in the sixth meditation, but the earlier meditations upon which it rests.

▶ Outstanding problems

It would seem to be a problem for Descartes that his argument relies on God not being a deceiver, because if God is not a deceiver, why in fact are we deceived so often? Descartes argues that this is an inevitable result of two facts. First, we are finite in our intelligence, so we cannot always be right. Second, the mind is only connected to the body via a small part of the brain (the pineal gland), so the information it gets from the body comes indirectly, via the various nerves in the body. For every sense perception, there is a series of causes. Nerve A will send the signal to nerve B and so on until it finally reaches the mind at, say, Z. Imagine such a sequence: A–B–D–G–M–Z. If the sequence starts at D but continues the same, the mind will receive a signal identical to that which would normally be sent when the series starts at A. In such a case, if A is the end of my toe, I will feel as though the end of my toe is in pain, even though it has not been touched. Descartes says there is no way around this: it is an inevitable result of the way in which our minds are connected to our bodies. We should just be grateful that God has given us a way of sensing which is in normal circumstances reliable.

However, it must be said that while Descartes explains well why we do make mistakes, he hasn't really answered the question of why God didn't see fit to design us a little better. The possibility of error does seem to be inevitable, but only because of the way we happen to have been designed. God must surely take ultimate responsibility for this and, as a consequence, also for our errors.

One final matter outstanding is a solution to the dreaming argument. Descartes now declares – contrary to his pronouncements in the first meditation – that there is a feature which distinguishes dreaming from waking: dream experiences are not linked by memory to other experiences. This raises two questions, one serious, one less so. First, dream experiences do *seem* to be part of a connected series of memories, so can't we be dreaming and it only *seem* to us that our experiences are connected by memory to other experiences? The new answer to the dreaming problem doesn't seem to provide a convincing solution. Second, if it is so easy to refute the dreaming argument, why did he use it in the first place!

▶ Conclusion

Descartes has come to the end of his project. There is a symmetry in the *Meditations*. He starts the book as someone who carries with him a body of beliefs he thinks he knows. He slowly attacks these until he is left with nothing but the certainty of his own existence. Then, he slowly builds up his beliefs once more until he ends up back where he started – convinced of the existence of himself, God and the material world, but this time convinced on the basis of what he takes to be sound foundations.

The book is in some ways a metaphor for a lot of philosophy. It leaves the world as it is, while at the same time utterly transforming it. Philosophers often believe much the same things as everyone else. But their reflections lead them to base these beliefs on considerations that others are often unaware of, or to see the world in a slightly different way.

In this and many other ways, the *Meditations* is an exemplary philosophical text. You may disagree with almost all of it, but when you've finished reading it, you will almost certainly understand yourself, the world and philosophy better.

Summary

Descartes's goal in the *Meditations* is to establish a sure and certain **foundation** for his knowledge. To do this he follows the **method of doubt**. He decides to disregard all beliefs which he can doubt until he is left only with something certain. He rejects the evidence of his senses because they have in the past deceived him and have thus proven to be an unreliable source of knowledge. He also considers the possibility that he is dreaming and therefore may be tricked into thinking that everything that he thinks is real is just a chimera.

In dreams, at least some basic truths are beyond doubt. But if God were a deceiver, or if a powerful **evil demon** were deceiving him, he could be wrong even about this.

The only thing Descartes can't doubt is that he thinks and he exists. Reflecting on this, he concludes that he must be in **essence** a thinking, rather than physical thing, because although the idea of body can be separated from his existence, the idea of thought cannot. He confirms this by considering a piece of wax and concluding that it is his intellect which allows him to know its essence, not his senses. This shows that the intellect is primary.

Descartes knows that he exists because he **clearly and distinctly perceives** this to be true. Such perceptions would not make him certain, he concludes, unless they were true. Armed with this hallmark of certainty, he tries to establish whether God exists, for if he does, he can be sure he is not being deceived about even the most basic truths.

His first attempted proof of God is based on the **causal reality principle**: since the cause of the idea of God must be at least as perfect as the idea itself, so God must exist.

But then, why does God allow him to be in error? This is purely because God has made us as best he can: he has given us a finite **intellect**, but the **will** does not admit of degree so we had to have it complete. We err when our will asserts things to be true or false which are beyond the capacity of our intellect to accurately judge.

Descartes's second proof of the existence of God is a version of the **ontological argument**. This attempts to show that a non-existent God is a contradiction in terms and that therefore God must exist as certainly as a triangle must have three sides.

Descartes concludes the *Meditations* by arguing that material objects must exist. This is because the idea of material things comes from something outside of himself. This must be material things themselves or something else. Because nature leads him to expect the former and God would not deceive him, he can be sure that material objects exist. This completes the re-establishment of all Descartes's beliefs on a surer foundation – he hopes!

Glossary

Causal reality principle   The principle that nothing less perfect or complete can be the cause of something more perfect or complete.

Clear and distinct perception   When the mind apprehends something so evident that its truth cannot be doubted.

Essence   The essential nature of a thing – that which cannot be separated from the idea of it.

Evil demon   A device used to personify the possibility that we are constantly being deceived about even the simplest of apparent truths.

Intellect   The faculty with which we reason and which is finite in us, but infinite in God.

Foundationalism   An approach to philosophy which seeks to establish truth on a secure and certain basis.

Method of doubt   The systematic doubt of all beliefs in order to arrive at truths which are certain and indubitable.

Ontological argument   An argument that seeks to show that we can know God exists purely by thinking about what the idea of concept of God entails.

Will   The faculty which allows us to make free choices, which is single, indivisible and does not admit of degrees.

Further reading

John Cottingham's translation of the *Meditations on First Philosophy* (Cambridge University Press) is highly recommended especially since it comes accompanied by a selection of the objections and replies. Other than the *Meditations*, *The*

Discourse on Method is the next most important work by Descartes and is available in many editions, including F. E. Sutcliffe's translation (Penguin), which also includes the *Meditations*.

Cottingham also contributed the *Descartes* volume to the *Great Philosophers* series (Phoenix). The book manages to be clear while at the same time presenting a fresh picture of the sometimes tired, caricatured figure of Descartes. The book also appears as part of the anthology of the series, *The Great Philosophers*, edited by Ray Monk and Fredric Raphael (Phoenix).

3 David Hume: *An Enquiry concerning Human Understanding* (1748)

▶ Background

Perhaps the simplest way into Hume's *Enquiry concerning Human Understanding* (1748) is to contrast the author's empiricist approach with that of his rationalist predecessors, such as Descartes (see Chapter 2 on the *Meditations*). To put it rather crudely, empiricists believe that all knowledge is derived from experience, and there is nothing which can be understood by the mind alone. Without experience, the mind is, as Locke put it, a 'blank slate' (*tabula rasa*), incapable of thinking of anything.

This contrasts with the approach of rationalists such as Descartes, who believed that fundamental truths about reality could be discovered purely by thinking, without any reference to experience. Rationalists have high hopes for the power of *a priori* reasoning – reasoning that starts from basic principles of logic and rationality which can be known to be true without reference to experience.

The distinction between rationalism and empiricism can easily descend into caricature. It is not that rationalists see all experience as irrelevant and empiricists believe experience justifies all our beliefs. What one actually finds on reading these philosophers is that Descartes does base some of his arguments on the evidence of experience and Hume argues that some of the principles of thought we employ are not justified by experience. The major difference is that Descartes believed rationality was the ultimate underpinning of all our knowledge, whereas for Hume, experience, custom and habit are at least as important and often more so.

While distinctions such as that between rationalists and empiricists can help us get to grips with unfamiliar philosophy, when reading any work it is important not to allow preconceived notions about which school a philosopher is coming from to get in the way of understanding the arguments they actually put forward. This is particularly true for Hume, whose empiricism is far subtler than broad-brushed generalisations about empiricism would suggest were possible.

▶ The text

The story of Hume's *Enquiry* provides encouragement for anyone who has struggled to find an audience for their work. The book is effectively a rewrite of Part I of Hume's earlier *A Treatise of Human Nature* (1738). Although now regarded as a masterpiece, Hume recalls in his short memoir, *My Own Life*: 'Never literary attempt was more unfortunate than my *Treatise of Human Nature*. It fell dead-born from the press without reaching such distinction, as even to excite a murmur among the zealots.'

Hume believed the failure to be due to the manner rather than the matter of the book, and so several years after its failure he revisited Part I of the *Treatise* and the *Enquiry* was born. Alas, it was not much more successful. It would be many years before Hume would be acknowledged as perhaps the greatest British philosopher.

Hume himself saw the *Enquiry* as the superior, more polished work. Nevertheless, one often finds scholarly debate focuses on the longer *Treatise*. It would be a pity if this trend were to put people off reading the *Enquiry*, since it is a lucid, clear and compelling work, in many ways easier to navigate one's mind through than the lengthy *Treatise*.

▶ I   Of the different species of philosophy

The first section of the *Enquiry* sits apart from the remainder of the text. What follows is a sustained argument, leading into a detailed application of the principles Hume establishes to various areas of philosophy. Section I does not introduce either the main argument or these later themes, but rather reflects on the general nature of philosophy itself.

The dangers of reading a text two and a half centuries after it was written are evident in the book's first two words: 'moral philosophy'. Nowadays, we would take that to refer specifically to ethics, or the philosophy of judging the rights and wrongs of human conduct. However, for Hume the term simply contrasts with natural philosophy, which we would now call physical science. So what Hume goes on to say applies to most, if not all, of what we would now consider philosophy, not just ethics.

Hume distinguishes between two types of philosophy, that which considers humanity (or man, as Hume called it) as 'chiefly born for action' and that which considers it 'in the light of a reasonable rather than an active being'. The distinction Hume is really making is between two approaches to treating the subject of humanity: the evocative, emotional and pleasing on the one hand, and the analytic, rational and reasoned on the other.

The second is easier to understand, since it simply describes the philosophical approach to human nature. This approach seeks to understand humanity by cool, calm and careful reasoning. It aims to establish the most general principles possible which enable us to understand our place in the world. It doesn't seek to discover just *what* we know, but *how* we know it and what justifies the claim that we do know, rather than merely believe. It doesn't seek simply to distinguish right from wrong but to establish the principles which allow us to judge between right and wrong. It doesn't seek merely to represent the huge edifice of human nature, creativity, ethics and intellect, but to understand the foundations on which it rests.

So noble an enterprise may seem beyond reproach. But in a way, the whole of this first section is a pre-emptive defence of philosophy against its critics. The problem, as Hume explains, is that this kind of approach to human nature leads us into difficult arguments and abstract reasoning. From a distance, the relevance of these arguments may be hard to discern. Philosophers can look like strange eccentrics who are obsessed by matters of irrelevant detail. Compared to the poet's treatment of human loss and triumph, for example, philosophy can appear sterile, dry and irrelevant. It appears to have no use or purpose to anyone other than aficionados of abstract reasoning.

In contrast, the first type of philosophy Hume describes is obviously relevant to the concerns of people in general. This kind of philosophy never strays too far from everyday concerns, since it aims merely to 'represent the common sense of mankind in more beautiful and engaging colours'. Although Hume's description makes this sound more like poetry than philosophy, the examples he gives of practitioners of this art are all essayists, if not fully-fledged philosophers. Cicero, La Bruyère and Addison are identified as authors of this lesser style of philosophy, while Aristotle, Malebranche and Locke are exemplars of the better, though less obviously engaging style. Interestingly, the philosophers Hume identifies as being greater, but less well thought of, are now considered giants of philosophy, whereas the popular thinkers of his time have largely been forgotten. Posterity, it seems, has been a better judge of quality in philosophy than Hume's peers.

Hume is describing a dispute which still continues today. It is basically about the accusation that philosophy is removed from the concerns of everyday life and much poorer for it. For instance, the noted journalist Simon Jenkins wrote, of the great twentieth-century philosopher W. V. O. Quine: 'Quine's work was not a window on the Great Beyond but an intellectual microscope applied to games he played with others' (*The Times*, 3 January 2001). As evidence, Jenkins points out that he had 'understood hardly a word' of Quine's obituary.

Hume's defence of what he thought of as the best philosophy could be used in response to Jenkins today. Hume argues that such philosophy relies on making very careful and subtle arguments. Hence, its practitioners are likely to get it wrong often, and thus can easily be made to look stupid. Also, because their reasoning goes into great depth and it is many stages removed from the point at which the questions first arise in the general population, it is easy for their work to appear abstract and irrelevant. Even its practitioners find that their reasonings do not apply directly to everyday life and can separate out their philosophical reflections from daily living.

Philosophy matters because only careful and thorough thought can lead us to reject the many false beliefs and ideas we would otherwise be encumbered with. Philosophy is also important because the questions it considers are so fundamental. Only philosophy turns the eye of enquiry inwards on to the mind of the thinker itself, for instance, enabling us to understand not just how to categorise objects in the world, but also the 'operations of the mind'. It is a shallow thinker who rejects such concerns as irrelevant.

Hume's defence does, however, grant something to the other species of philosophy he criticises. That does at least have the virtue of being clear, engaging and accessible. Hume's hope is that his own work will combine the rigour of the best form of philosophy with the colour and vitality of its more vulgar relation. Many would say he succeeded.

▶ II Of the origin of ideas

The starting point of the *Enquiry* proper is an investigation into the fundamental basis of knowledge. In this respect, Hume follows the same 'foundationalist' strategy as Descartes. The difference is that whereas Descartes searched for these foundations within his own mind, Hume looked for them in his experience of the world.

Hume, like Locke, believed that knowledge starts with what we are directly aware of, which are the contents of our own mind – what he called the 'perceptions of the mind'. Hume puts these perceptions into two categories: ideas and impressions. Impressions are what we perceive when we look at an object, feel a sensation or emotion, touch something and so on. Impressions can thus be of things external or internal to ourselves. Ideas are what we perceive when we imagine, think of, or remember something. Impressions, he says, are 'forcible and lively', whilst ideas are 'faint and dull'. In common speech, we may refer to 'ideas' as 'thoughts' and 'impressions' as 'sensations' (though note Hume's particular definitions of each). 'The most lively thought', he claims, 'is still inferior to the dullest sensation.'

Here, Hume could mean one of two things. Firstly, he could mean that *all* ideas are less lively than *all* impressions. This seems clearly false. I can just catch sight of something in the distance through the fog and have a very faint impression of it, whilst I can dream something very vividly indeed. What Hume more likely means is that any particular idea will always be less vivid than the impression from which it originally derived (as he claims all ideas are derived from impressions). But even this may be false on occasion. In a traumatic experience, I may not be aware of many things going on around me as I struggle to survive. However, once the original trauma has passed, these things may return in my memories more vividly than my original experience of them.

This problem highlights a general difficulty in Hume's account. It seems that by making vivacity and liveliness what distinguishes an idea from an impression, he has not selected the defining distinguishing features of either. Although it is true that most ideas are less vivid than impressions, this does not capture their essential nature, but is rather a consequence of their essential nature. What truly distinguishes them is that impressions are the raw data of experience and ideas are later copies of this data. Usually, a copy is less vivid than the original. But it is not this feature which distinguishes a copy from an original. A copy of an old painting may, for example, be more vivid. So Hume seems to make two mistakes. First, he confuses typical features of ideas and impressions with their natures. But second, if vivacity is how we are supposed to distinguish ideas from impressions, he also turns a useful rule of thumb (copies are *usually* less detailed than originals) into a strict rule (copies are *always* less detailed than originals).

Why did Hume do this? The reason is probably that he wanted to be able to distinguish ideas and impressions and *then* make the claim that all ideas are derived from impressions. If he simply *defined* ideas as copies of impressions, he would be beginning his theory with a bold hypothesis, rather than with facts based clearly on experience.

Whatever his errors, is he right to claim that all ideas derive from impressions? We can see how ideas of dragons and other fanciful creatures can be amalgams of parts we have already experienced. But what about ideas such as that of God? Hume claims this is just made up of ideas from experience augmented. For example, the idea of God's infinite goodness comes from impressions of limited goodness, which we then just imagine without end. This makes it clear that ideas are not simply copies of impressions. They are impressions copied, augmented, modified and/or rearranged. It is difficult to think of an idea which *could not* be explained in this way. But the question is *are* they formed in such a way? It is possible, for example, to derive the idea of atoms by simply adapting impressions, but is that actually how the idea arose? It is very difficult, if not impossible to tell. So whilst Hume could be right, he hasn't given us convincing reasons to believe he must be right.

There are other problems too. Russell points out how the so called 'rules of thought', the principles of logic and induction, are not given to us by experience, but are *a priori* (see Chapter 4 on *The Problems of Philosophy*). In this case, at least some ideas are not derived from experience. Hume returns to induction later.

The final problem is one Hume himself considers. If we were to arrange all the shades of blue in a row, remove one, and show them to someone who had never seen that shade, could she not imagine what that missing shade would look like? Hume concedes she could, but claims 'this instance is so singular, that it is scarcely worth our observing'. This may seem to be a poor response, because it is clear that one counter-example is enough to destroy a claim of the sort 'all Xs are Ys'. However, it is revealing, because it suggests that Hume is not bothered that he hasn't got an exceptionless rule. He seems content enough to have discovered regularities in nature that hold for the most part. For an empiricist, who seeks to understand the world as it is given to experience, it would perhaps be foolish to assume that all regularities have to be exceptionless. If experience shows they are not, experience wins, not prior suppositions.

One might think an easy way to solve the problem of the missing shade is to say that it is a modification of the other shades rather than a distinct idea. But this would not do, since by that reasoning all colours can be placed in a spectrum and be seen as mere modifications of the next shade, and so all colours would be modifications of one colour. This seems absurd.

Hume's basic claim that all ideas derive from impressions thus faces serious difficulties. First, his idea–impression distinction seems to be wrongly characterised as hinging on the distinction between the liveliness and dullness of these 'perceptions of the mind'. Second, his claim that all ideas derive from impressions also seems to have several counter-examples. Perhaps Hume needs to say more about the relation between experience and ideas, or maybe his theory is more fundamentally flawed.

▶ III   Of the association of ideas

Hume claims that there is clearly some 'principle of connexion between the different thoughts or ideas of the mind'. Thoughts do not come from nowhere. No matter how loosely our thoughts appear to flow, there is always some hidden connexion between them. Hume believed there are only three basic types of connexion: resemblance, contiguity (closeness) in time or place, and cause or effect. If we examine the flow of our ideas, it will always be possible to explain the jump from one to another in terms of one of these relations.

This is a hard claim to deny or verify. We can probably work out some connexion between any two ideas based on these three principles, but how can we know whether that is the actual connexion? This is a problem shared with the impressions–ideas theory, which again is plausible, but almost impossible to test. It is perhaps ironic that we have already found two major planks of Hume's theory that seem to be untestable when the most common characterisation of empiricism is that it is based on the principle that ideas can be tested against experience.

▶ IV   Sceptical doubts concerning the operations of the understanding

Part I

The principle which opens this section has come to be known as Hume's Fork. This is a distinction which Hume believed should be made (but which often is not) between two fundamentally different objects of reason: relations of ideas and matters of fact. Relations of ideas include algebra, geometry and logic – all those areas of knowledge where affirmations can be demonstrably true and certain, because they are basically no more than affirmations about the relations of ideas: $1 + 1 = 2$ can never be wrong, because no matter how the world is, the ideas represented in this sum are such that they have to be related in this way.

Matters of fact include propositions such as, 'the cat on the mat is fat,' and 'the world began with a big bang'. The truth or falsity of these ideas cannot be ascertained merely by attending to the ideas contained in the proposition. No matter how long one considers the idea of the world, one will never reach *a priori* the conclusion that it must have begun with a big bang. Hence, it is a feature of statements of fact that their opposites are always logically possible and contain no contradiction. 'The sun won't rise tomorrow' is not a self-contradictory statement; $1 + 1 = 3$ is.

Hume next claims that: 'All reasoning concerning matters of fact seems to be founded on the relation of cause and effect.' In this he seems to be correct. Our belief that the sun will rise tomorrow rests on the assumption that the forces which caused it to rise yesterday will operate again tomorrow. Even the belief that the cat on the mat is fat depends upon the assumption that the cat's appearance is an effect of the way it actually is.

The next question therefore is, 'How do we arrive at the knowledge of cause and effect?' The answer is, 'not by reason, but by experience'. There is no way that we could, just by observing a sequence of events, deduce *a priori* that earlier events were causing later ones, or that an object with certain properties also has other causal properties (for example, that clear water can cause a person to suffocate). Again, this can be demonstrated by the fact that there is no logical contradiction in imagining events occurring without or with different causes or effects. If apples defying gravity is not a logical contradiction, then it cannot be by logic that we conclude they must obey gravity. If clouds forming for no reason is not a logical contradiction, then it cannot be by logic that we conclude clouds must form for a reason. Therefore, it is experience alone that gives us knowledge of cause and effect, and not reason.

Part II

Hume has concluded that all reasoning concerning matters of fact depends upon the relation of cause and effect and that our knowledge of the relation of cause and effect is founded on experience, not reason. The next question, then, must be: 'What is the foundation of all conclusions from experience?'

Hume's answer is largely negative: conclusions from experience are not founded on reasoning. This is a mightily sceptical claim. It means that the ideas that bread nourishes, water freezes at zero degrees centigrade, and all men are mortal and so on are not based on reason. Why does Hume believe this? Objects in nature, he claims, have certain powers which are hidden from us. Bread has the power to nourish, for example, but we cannot in any sense observe that power. We can only find that it has it when we eat it. No matter how much bread we have eaten, when we see a new loaf, we cannot observe that power to nourish. We assume it has it, but this is just an assumption based on past experience. It is not based on reasoning.

This is a surprising claim, but Hume supports it by asking us to consider the nature of arguments based on experience, such as this one:

> I have found that such an object has always been attended with such an effect. I foresee that other objects, which are, in appearance similar, will be attended with similar effects.

This is clearly not a valid deduction – the conclusion in the second sentence does not follow from the premise in the first. In order to make the argument valid, a second premise is required, along the lines of:

> Whenever such an object has always been attended with such an effect, objects which are in appearance similar will continue to be attended with a similar effect.

This is a premise which Hume claims neither reason nor experience can ever justify. (Compare Russell's attempt to provide the missing premise in *The Problems of Philosophy*.) Experience, being confined to the past, can never provide proof for what the future will be like. Nor can reason justify this premise, since it is not contrary to reason to deny that it is true. The gap is just as gaping if we attempt to show that the conclusion of this argument is probable.

Just because Hume cannot provide the missing premise, it doesn't prove no-one ever could. However, as even animals, idiots and children learn from experience, and clearly don't employ anything like this missing premise when they do so, it seems clear that no such deductive argument is employed in our actual learning from experience.

However, we certainly do reason along the lines of the invalid argument set out above, which is an example of *induction*. How we do so is the subject of the next section.

▶ V Sceptical solution of these doubts

Part I

After extolling the virtues of sceptical philosophy (by which Hume means what we would call modern Western philosophy), Hume considers how we reason concerning matters of fact. He observes that our philosophical reasonings are incapable of undermining our 'reasonings of common life'. For example, nothing Hume has said so far has stopped him believing the sun *will* rise tomorrow, even though there are no strictly rational reasons for believing this. It seems that nature, of which human beings are for Hume very much a part, has made sure of this. To find out how nature does this, Hume conducts a thought experiment.

Imagine someone were brought into the world for the first time, fully equipped with all the normal faculties of reason and reflection. Looking around, he would see a succession of events, but would never be able to see the causal powers which link them nor form a rational argument that would show that earlier events cause later ones. This merely repeats Hume's earlier point about the inability of reason and observation to tell us anything about causation. But, if this person were to continue to garner more experience and had observed similar objects or events to constantly follow each other, he would soon begin to infer the existence of one object from the appearance of the other. Yet it is not by reason that he infers this, but by custom or habit. Repetition makes him expect the 'effect' to follow the 'cause', not any process of rational thought. Custom is nature's great teacher, without which we would be lost.

It follows from all this that 'all belief of matter of fact or real existence is derived merely from some object, present to the memory or senses, and a customary conjunction between that and some other object'. Belief in cause and effect therefore depends upon the psychological effect of witnessing constant conjunction – two objects or events repeatedly following one another, or being found together. It is not something we either directly observe or discover by a rational process.

Part II

Hume now turns to the nature of beliefs and the customary conjunctions between them. The mind is free to think of ideas in any way it sees fit. You can imagine a winged horse as easily as a normal one. But what the mind is not free to do is to imagine a winged horse and really believe it to have existed. So although the ideas of winged and normal horses can just as easily be thought of as each other, there is a certain *feeling* attached to *genuine beliefs* which is absent in *ideas of fictions*. Ideas which we truly believe are involuntary, strong, immediate and are held by force of custom. Ideas of fiction are weaker, and there is no necessity to our having them. So it is the *manner* in which we have ideas, rather than the ideas themselves, which distinguishes beliefs from mere fictions. Whether or not our beliefs are true or not is, however, another question.

From where does this strong manner in which we have beliefs derive? Hume claims it comes from custom. Nature, as he has said, has established connections among particular ideas, namely those of contiguity, resemblance and cause and effect. When objects are presented to the senses or memory, these connections are strengthened, such that they are stronger than they could be if they were just imagined. And the more the objects are presented to us, the stronger the associations will be. Various examples show this. If I look at a picture of someone I know, then there is my idea of the person, the present impression of the picture and the relation of resemblance between them. Where there is a good likeness in the picture, my idea of that person is strengthened by this resemblance, whereas if there is little likeness, my idea of the person will be more faint. Thus it is that the vivacity of our ideas and the strength of the relations between them are both increased by objects presented to the senses much more than they can by mere imagination. *How* this is so, we do not know, but Hume is sure *that* it is so.

However, it should be pointed out that error can occur. Two objects can be presented together and associated in my mind with all the forcefulness of a belief, even though those objects have no real relation at all. Such is often the case with phobias. If we come to associate a harmless object with something fearful, we will begin to fear the harmless object. In this case, we can form a false belief that something harmless is dangerous. Thus, we cannot know if our beliefs are true by their vivacity and the strengths of their association in our mind, and Hume doesn't here provide an alternative test of truth and falsehood, although he does return to this issue in Section VII.

Hume has thus provided us with an explanation of how we reason concerning matters of fact through custom, not reason, and shown us why this is necessary. Whether this is enough to dispel the scepticism of Section IV is for us to decide, but even if it is not, he has some more interesting things to say on the subject after he deals with the question of probability.

▶ VI Of probability

Locke distinguished between demonstrative and probable arguments. Demonstrative arguments concern maths, geometry and so on, whilst probable arguments concern things such as the rising of the sun. This distinction mirrors the two prongs of Hume's fork. Hume, however, wishes to divide matters of fact into two categories: proofs and probabilities. Those matters of fact of which there can be no doubt (even though they are not logically demonstrable), such as the existence of gravity, are considered proven. Probability concerns matters of fact for which such proofs are not possible because of a lack of constant conjunction.

So what is probability? If chance means that an effect is not the inevitable result of its cause, then Hume says chance does not exist. In cases of apparent chance, there is merely an ignorance of the real cause. So chance or probability arises when *apparently* identical causes have a number of different effects. Consider rolling a die. In truth, no one roll is identical to any other, but they appear to be basically the same. What we have found is that, over time, each result of the roll occurs one in six times. In saying, then, that there is a six-to-one chance of rolling a particular number in the future, we are merely projecting into the future the past proportion of outcomes. But for any given roll, it is inevitable, given the way the die was rolled, that the number ends up showing as it does.

What Hume is thus doing in this section is showing how, even though matters of fact are not logically demonstrable, we can distinguish between proofs and probabilities whilst at the same time retaining the idea that every occurrence is the determinate outcome of its cause.

▶ VII Of the idea of necessary connexion

Part I

All our ideas, Hume claims, come from an antecedent (prior) impression. And in order to fully understand that idea, we need to know what impression(s) it comes from. For example, knowing that the idea of a unicorn is a combination of impressions and that the idea of a tiger comes from whole impressions is part of what enables us to know one is a fiction and one is a fact (thus completing the unfinished account of this difference in Section V). So in order to fully understand the idea of necessary connexion, we need to locate the impression from which it derives. Hume has already argued that we do not perceive necessary connexion in the external world: all we perceive there is a series of constant conjunctions. So where does the idea come from? Hume considers three likely sounding candidates.

First, Hume considers the possibility that we directly observe the power of necessary connexion when we are aware of the power of our minds over our bodies. The thesis is that 'we are every moment conscious of internal power; while we feel that, by the simple command of our will, we can move the organs of our body'. Hume rejects this for three reasons. First, how can we directly observe this power when, in fact, the union of mind and body is the most mysterious thing in the entire universe? Second, we cannot move all parts of our body at will, and what is more, we discover which parts we can control and those we cannot by experience, not by any direct awareness of our power over them. Third, when we move an arm, for example, we in fact move various muscles and nerves between the arm and the brain first. Now, if we were directly aware of the power we had, we would have known this intuitively, whereas in fact we have to learn this from anatomy.

A second possibility is that we can feel the power of the mind over its own ideas. Every time we conjure up a new idea, we feel the power of necessary connexion. Hume also rejects this for three reasons. First, if we know a cause, we must know what power in the cause produces the effect. But we know so little about the mind that we cannot pretend to know any such thing in this case.

Second, the power of the mind over its ideas is limited, and those limits are only known by experience. (Compare this to the argument concerning the mind's power over the body.) Third, our power over our ideas varies according to our state of mind, health and so on. The only reasons we can offer for this fact are from experience, which again shows that the power itself is not known to us.

A third possibility, which Hume gives short shrift, is the theory of occasionalism. This is the idea that God is the cause of all events and is thus the power which makes a cause always produce an effect. This is a kind of non-explanation and Hume dismisses it because he cannot see how any chain of reasoning could lead us to this conclusion, as it would take us way beyond what we can justly infer from experience.

Part II

This part of the *Enquiry* is absolutely crucial. Many readers miss its significance, including those who should know better. At this point, we are left with the puzzle about where the idea of necessary connexion comes from. Hume has stressed that all ideas come from impressions and has so far failed to locate the impression which is the source of the idea of necessary connexion. This leads some to think that Hume is really saying we do not have an idea of necessary connexion at all, or that it is a fiction, since it has no corresponding impression. But, right here, Hume says explicitly what the impression is.

Nature has instilled in us the capacity to form the idea of necessary connexion from constant conjunction. How is this done? When we observe a constant conjunction, the idea or impression of the first event always conveys to our minds the idea of the subsequent event. The mind is carried from the idea of the cause to that of the effect. This is something which just happens to us, without our will. It is thus this necessity of moving from one thought to the other which gives us the impression from which the idea of necessary connexion derives. 'This connexion, therefore, which we feel in the mind, this customary transition of the imagination from one object to its usual attendant, is the sentiment or impression from which we form the idea of power or necessary connexion.' (I once had to show this sentence to a colleague writing a scholarly book on Hume to prove to him that Hume does locate an impression from which the idea of necessary connexion arises, so don't be surprised if you come across people writing on Hume who neglect this!)

This is important. It shows that the impression of necessary connexion arises in the mind. What we do is project this idea out on to the world and believe that there is necessary connexion in the world itself. It should also be noted that nowhere does Hume question that we are right to believe that there is such a thing as necessary connexion in the world – only that the origin of that idea comes from our own minds, not the world. Indeed, many of his arguments elsewhere depend upon the reality of cause and effect. This is also important, since some commentators claim that Hume denies the reality of causation. Hume seems to believe that the impression in the mind he has located is simply nature's way of teaching us about cause and effect. He does not deny that there is cause and effect in the world itself and that it is not just in the mind.

However, critics would argue that once Hume locates the source of our idea of cause and effect as the operation of the mind, the door to scepticism is wide open, and it would seem natural to doubt the objective reality of cause and effect. One way out for Hume would be to admit, which he does not for the reasons already given, that we do have some direct experience of physical necessity. Perhaps Hume's claim that all experience must be of particular impressions is at fault here. It may be possible to explain how we observe the power of causation in some way which does not require there to be a particular impression of this power.

▶ VIII   Of liberty and necessity

Part I

Hume notes there is a continued disagreement over whether or not human action is free or not. He concludes that the only reason for this disagreement is that the terms themselves, 'freedom', 'liberty', 'necessity' and so on are not properly defined. He wagers that if we could all agree on what these terms mean, all our apparent disagreements would disappear. Hume thus claims the controversy is merely verbal, rather than factual.

The meaning of a word, for Hume, is given by the idea in the mind to which the word is attached. This is a very contentious theory, since if meanings are determined by ideas private to each individual, how can we have shared meanings for words which make communication possible? However, we should not worry too much about this since Hume's basic claim that the disagreement is verbal does not depend on his particular theory of meaning.

Hume first considers necessity and reminds us that it is constant conjunction which gives us this idea. In the affairs of people, he argues, we also observe constant conjunctions. There is uniformity in human behaviour and action over time and place, so strong that if we were to be told of a society hugely different from ours, where people were not jealous, ambitious and so on, we would disbelieve it as much as we would stories about dragons and monsters. The differences in human behaviour also teach us the influence of factors such as age, sex and culture have on behaviour, in just the same way that differences in the behaviour of matter teach us about the influences of temperature, air pressure and so on.

It is true that human behaviour is unpredictable. But this is not, as the 'vulgar' believe, a result of any uncertainty in the cause, but rather 'the secret opposition of contrary causes'. This is the same in persons as it is in matter. If a telephone explodes, we believe it was caused by something not usually operative in telephones, and if a patient man gets angry, we assume there is some reason for this which is not usually operative.

Hume gives more examples to support his case and concludes: 'The conjunction between motives and voluntary actions is as regular and uniform as that between the cause and effect in any part of nature', a fact, he claims, which 'has been universally acknowledged'. We do not think that people act randomly, but that their actions are explained by their motives, dispositions, desires and so on.

But does this resolve the dispute as he claimed it would? Perhaps not. The real dispute is not over whether motives cause action, but whether motives and so on are themselves effects of other causes. If this is the case, then the originating causes of actions lie not within our own minds, but in our environment and our genes. This is what determinists believe, and not everyone agrees with them. We might agree that desires and motives are part of what cause actions, but disagree about whether these themselves are chosen or whether, in addition to these, there is an extra faculty of 'free will' which makes the final choice. Hume's argument is therefore incomplete. However, Hume does outline the basis of the compatibilist approach to determinism. That is to say, it is claimed that the fact that all human actions are effects of motives, character and so on, which are in turn effects of other causes, *ad infinitum* does not contradict the principle of human freedom, which is that we have '*a power of acting or not acting, according to the determinations of the will*; that is, if we choose to remain at rest, we may; if we choose to move, we may also.' However, if we take the more usual definition of human freedom, which is that 'men are free only if they could have done otherwise', Hume has not shown we are free in this way, although there are problems with this notion.

If, as Hume claims, no-one fundamentally disagrees as to the facts of the matter, why do we seem to disagree? Hume's explanation is that we tend to reason (perhaps not consciously) as follows:

1   We perceive necessary connexion in nature.
2   We do not perceive any necessity forcing our own actions.
3   Therefore, we have a liberty of action which nature does not.

Hume, as we have seen denies (1). We do not perceive any necessary connexion in nature, only a constant conjunction. And, as Hume has eloquently argued, such constant conjunctions are to be found in human action as well. To disagree with Hume we could either reject his account of causation, or reject his claim that human behaviour is as regular as the behaviour of bodies in nature.

Part II

What are the consequences of accepting this position? Does it mean that no one is to blame for their actions? Even if the theory did have dangerous consequences, that would not in itself refute the theory. But Hume claims that it does not have such consequences anyway. He believes that without the causal link between motives, character and action, we would have no basis for punishment, blame or the idea of repentance. It only makes sense to punish someone if their character is somehow the cause of their actions. If it were not, then there would be nothing to punish or reform. So Hume argues that we actually need the idea of necessary connexion to apply to human action to justify our morality.

The other main problem is that if everything is an effect, eventually God will be found to be the initial cause. As there are many bad things done in the world, this either means God is to blame for everything or he is not wholly good. One way to avoid this is to claim that as a whole, the universe is good, even though individual parts may seem bad. Though Hume acknowledges that psychologically this belief fails, in that it provides no comfort for a person suffering, none the less philosophically it makes sense. As regards the idea that God is the author of all things bad, Hume dodges the issue, arguing that 'there are mysteries, which mere natural and unassisted reason is very unfit to handle'. But in a way, Hume's evasion is justified. After all, he has consistently argued that matters of fact can only be known from experience. God's authorship of the universe is a matter of fact which cannot be known *a priori*. And as we have no direct experience of God either, we are unfit to reason about him in any detail.

Of course, this argument not only saves God from being blamed as the author of all sin, but it also prevents his nature and existence being the just subject of philosophy too, a consequence the tactful Hume fails to point out. It should also be noted that in Hume's time it was prudent not to question too vigorously orthodox religious doctrine.

▶ IX Of the reason of animals

Do animals reason? To answer this, as with any other question concerning matters of fact, we have to use a combination of experience and analogy. If we discover that an animal has a heart, for example, and that such an organ circulates the blood in all other animals we have studied, we should reason until shown otherwise that this is also the function of the heart in this animal. In the same way, we should conclude that animals do reason.

There are two facts which together suggest animals do have the power of reason. First, animals learn from experience. This shows, according to Hume, that animals, like humans, reach conclusions about more than they are actually aware of in sense experience, and that this process of inference is a matter of using experience of the past as a guide to what will happen in the future. In other words, animals reason as we do.

Second, this reasoning cannot be based on any process of argument. Seeing as Hume has already claimed that we do not use any such principle of argument in our reasoning concerning experience, it is hard to suppose that an animal, a less sophisticated creature, has access to this form of reasoning that eludes us.

Hume is aware that people ascribe much animal behaviour to instinct. Hume's answer here is that we too have instinct: our capacity to learn from experience is itself an instinct, which we do not need to be taught about and, indeed, has no logical basis.

The differences between animal intelligence and our own are explained in the same way as differences in human intelligence are. These are factors such as capacity for attention, memory, distinguishing a number of causes, ability to carry a chain of reasoning further and so on. Hume provides a comprehensive list at the end of this section. The key point is that the difference between human and animal reasoning is a difference in degree, not of kind.

Much of what Hume said was ahead of its time. But in other respects, it may be a little crude. Modern psychology has shown there are many ways of learning, such as simple conditioning, whereas Hume supposes all learning from experience is a specie of induction. However, in emphasising how much we have in common with animals, Hume anticipated much of what later came to be received opinion.

▶ **X   Of miracles**

Part I

In all matters of fact, where there is disagreement, we must simply balance up the evidence for the one belief against the evidence for the other. 'A weaker evidence cannot destroy a stronger.' If gravity appears to always operate, we cannot deny the truth of gravity just because an illusionist like David Copperfield appears to be flying around the theatre.

The testimony of people is no exception to this rule. A person's testimony, though we may have no reason to believe that person to be a liar, must be balanced against all the evidence which contradicts what they say, which includes the testimony of others, experience and the character of the teller. Of course, sometimes we may be wrong, but this is always possible with matters of fact. Hume points out that the fabled Indian, who didn't believe in the stories of ice which he was told about, reasoned justly, as all of his experience of water and the effect of cooling on matter told against the idea that water would expand and solidify at one crucial temperature. He was wrong, but he reasoned as best as he could, given the information available to him.

However, even in this case, ice was something merely extraordinary, not truly miraculous. Ice was beyond his experience, but not contrary to it. For something to be miraculous, it must be 'a violation of the laws of nature'. Not everyone would agree with Hume. Many modern Christians would believe that a miracle can be merely a highly unlikely event occurring at a particularly apt time, even though it is not contrary to the laws of nature. For example, there are explanations of how the Red Sea could have parted according to natural laws, but is it not still a miracle that it happened just when Moses and the Israelites needed it to? But this is not satisfactory. To distinguish a remarkable coincidence from a miracle, we need some kind of idea of God's intervention. And if God intervened, it meant that he must have altered the progress of nature. And to do this, he must in some sense break the laws of nature, as nature alone would not have provided sufficient cause for the miracle. So Hume does seem to be right.

We can therefore have no reason to accept a miracle unless evidence for the miracle is greater than the evidence against it. Note, however, that we could still believe in miracles as an act of faith, one which would actually be contrary to reason. This makes the act of faith that much harder.

Part II

Hume continues his argument by claiming that, as a matter of fact, no miracle can ever be supported by reason. He gives four explanations for this. They all hinge on the key idea that the evidence for a law of nature, supported by all experience, can never be outweighed by a few conflicting experiences or testimonies. First, there is no-one so virtuous that they could never be free from the suspicion that they were deceiving. Second, the emotions of surprise and wonder are very strong, and such is their effect that we really want to believe in the extraordinary. Thus, humans are very susceptible to belief in apparent miracles. (This is important, because so far, Hume has based his argument against miracles on facts concerning how we actually do reason from experience. But as people clearly do believe in miracles, he has to explain why they do so when it is contrary to their normal method of reasoning.) Third, it is no coincidence that tales of miracles are most rife in 'primitive' and 'ignorant' societies (or, indeed, that aliens only seem to visit isolated farmhouses!). The more advanced we are in our intelligence and science, the less we believe in such things. Fourth, against the witnesses of any miracle, we can balance up an infinite number of witnesses to events which uphold the laws of nature. As laws of nature are by their very nature exceptionless, the whole of human history is, in effect, testimony against the reality of miracles.

Hume follows this up with a lengthy, interesting, though philosophically unimportant series of anecdotes to back up his arguments. He considers various reported cases of miracles, applies his ideas to them and discredits them. His conclusions, though, are worth noting. He argues that 'a miracle can never be proved so as to be the foundation of a system of religion'. Although he concludes that faith may yet provide a basis for belief in miracles and religion, since belief in the former is contrary to reason, the implication is clearly that belief in miracles has no place in religion.

▶ XI Of a particular providence and of a future state

In this section, Hume suddenly becomes coy, presenting his argument as if it were simply the recollection of what his friend attributes to be the thoughts of Epicurus (341–270 BCE). The odd-sounding title of this section refers to the belief that the world has been designed, with a particular purpose, by God. Hume argues that there is no *philosophical* justification for this belief. In doing so, he claims not to be undermining the foundations of society, but arguing for principles which any person arguing consistently must accept to be true.

Hume's target is the so-called 'argument from design' or 'teleological' argument for God's existence, which really contains three steps. The first is the observation that there is order in nature. The second is that this order contains the marks of intelligence and design, and that mere chance or the 'blind and unguided force of matter' is not causally sufficient to create this order. The conclusion is that therefore it must be God who created the world. Just as one infers the existence of a watchmaker from the order one finds in a watch, so one infers a creator from the order one finds in the universe.

Hume criticises this argument on the grounds that 'when we infer any particular cause from an effect, we must proportion the one to the other, and can never be allowed to ascribe to the cause any qualities, but what are exactly sufficient to produce the effect'. In other words, we can only infer a cause sufficient to produce the effect. For example, if a hole is blasted through a wall, we may only infer that the blast was sufficient to produce that hole. Though it *may* have been greater, we have no reason to claim that it *was* greater.

So, if we allow that the gods created the universe, we can only ascribe to them those powers sufficient to create the universe and no more. However, what the argument from design does is to claim that the existence of the universe points to an all-powerful, all-knowing, all-loving God. This is to endow God with more properties than are required to create the universe. (Now, with advances in physics, it is considered possible to ascribe *nothing* to the cause of the universe, it could actually be a *causa sui* – a cause of itself.) People make the mistake of positing the creator, and then becoming so enamoured of their own idea that they attribute many other qualities to it.

So, in essence, what Hume's argument does is not to attack the basic premise that there is order in the universe, but that from this order we can infer that God is its creator. He attacks this supposition as 'uncertain and useless'. Uncertain, because it goes beyond what we can reasonably infer from human experience, and useless, because it is based entirely on the order of nature, so we cannot use the 'discovery' that God exists to understand this order more. God's existence is derived from this order, so to attempt to derive new facts about this order from God's existence would be to reason in a circle.

Now, he considers a counter-argument from analogy. If it is right to infer from a half-finished building that there has been a builder, or from one footprint in the sand that someone has been walking there and the other prints must have been washed away, isn't it just as valid to argue from the order of the universe to an intelligent creator? Hume replies that we can infer in the analogous cases, because we know from experience the relation between human artefacts and human artisans, footprints and people. As all knowledge of matters of fact is based on experience, this is how we justify our inferences. But where we have seen only one example of something, with no previous knowledge of who or what created it, little or nothing can justly be drawn from experience about the nature of its creator. As there is some wisdom and goodness in nature, these can be ascribed to the creator, and so on. But we are very limited in how much we can ascribe to the creator, as we have no experience of other of its creations.

Later, Hume suggests that even this would be to ascribe too much. As we have no experience of God at all, and as the universe is a singular, unique thing, we cannot reason anything about its creator, as this would be to go way beyond how we can justly reason concerning matters of fact. Without experience of the universe's cause, there is no basis for any inference about it.

A final point is that just because reasonings such as the argument from design *should not* influence people's thoughts, that doesn't mean they *do not* influence them. The argument from design had, and still has, many supporters, despite Hume's devastating and seemingly unanswerable objections.

▶ XII Of the academical or sceptical philosophy

In this final section, Hume attempts to find the right role for scepticism in philosophy and avoid some of scepticism's more negative features. In Part I he considers scepticism concerning the existence of external objects. In Part II, he considers scepticism concerning our reasoning in matters of fact. In Part III he draws out what he believes are the right consequences of mitigated scepticism.

Part I

Hume distinguishes between antecedent and consequent scepticism. Antecedent scepticism, like that of Descartes, begins with universal doubt and then attempts to build up knowledge from those principles which are certain and cannot be doubted (see Chapter 2 on the *Meditations*.) This fails because, first, there are no such indubitable principles, and second, even if such a principle could be found, nothing could be built on it without using those faculties (reason, etc.) which we are supposed to already doubt.

Consequent scepticism is when we become sceptical because, having already reasoned, we discover faults and errors in our faculties, be they mental or perceptual. Perceptual error in itself does not justify universal doubt, as all this shows is that we must not trust our senses alone. Nor can this scepticism convince us that the external world does not exist.

However, Hume thinks 'the slightest philosophy' can destroy our certainty about external objects, as it teaches us that 'nothing can ever be present to the mind but an image of perception'. In other words, he believes reason leads to the belief that we do not directly perceive objects in the world. It is impossible to show that our perceptions resemble real objects, as we can only reason from experience, and experience is only ever of these perceptions. Nor can belief in God help us. Clearly, God does not make sure we are never deceived by our senses, so if sensory deception is OK by God, then we cannot argue from the fact of his goodness to the veracity of our experiences.

This antecedent scepticism is also reinforced by the collapse of the primary and secondary qualities distinction. Locke argued that, though secondary qualities such as smell, colour and taste were dependent on our senses, primary qualities such as extension, hardness and so on were not. But Hume rightly points out that knowledge of even these primary qualities depends on our senses, so we cannot consistently claim that primary qualities are independent of us if we say this is not true of secondary qualities.

Hume concludes by claiming that the belief in external objects faces a two-pronged challenge. If it rests on natural instinct, it is contrary to reason, as reason shows we do not directly perceive external objects. If it rests on reason, it is contrary to natural instinct, and at the same time fails to find this rational support, as there are no reasonable grounds for believing we experience external objects. What we are then left with is the view that such a belief is contrary to reason, and that all we are aware of are sensible qualities (i.e. qualities we perceived), and that once we take these away, there are no other properties left which we can ascribe to matter. It is merely, as Berkeley put it, 'something, I know not what'.

Part II

Hume now turns to attack the use of abstract reason to discover properties of reality, such as space and time. Hume shows that, if we try and reason about matters of fact just by using our powers of reason, we end up with contradictions. For instance, Zeno's famous paradoxes of motion seem to show that if space and time are infinitely divisible, it would be impossible for anything to move. But if we suppose they are not infinitely divisible, we have to suppose that each point of space is 'infinitely less than any real part of extension', since if this were not true, they would be divisible. But this is absurd, as an infinite number of non-extended points cannot be extended, yet space and time are extended.

Hume uses these examples to show how using pure logic to solve questions concerning real existence leads to absurdity and contradiction. In matters of fact, he claims there are no real abstract ideas, 'only particular ones, attached to a general term'. Abstract ideas belong to the realm of the relations of ideas.

This seems to open up another route for scepticism. Popular scepticism just claims we are fallible, so we should be sceptical, which is a weak form of scepticism. But philosophical scepticism reasons that matters of fact are only known through experience, and experiences depend upon cause and effect, which is in itself not supported by experience. In short, the sceptic reasons as Hume does, but concludes that this means our reasonings concerning matters of fact are worthless. Hume, on the other hand, believes that this view cannot result in any good, and therefore it is useless. Hume advocates just accepting how we reason and not giving in to excessive scepticism. Hume's argument is not a logical one, but a psychological and pragmatic one. As the complete suspension of belief advocated by the sceptic is neither possible nor desirable, we should simply carry on, aware of how we reason concerning matters of fact. This way of answering scepticism would also apply to the conclusions of Part I.

Part III

Hume calls this mitigated scepticism, that is, scepticism tempered by pragmatism. He believes this scepticism is useful for two reasons. First, it prevents dogmatism. Second, it will generally lead us to 'enquiries to such subjects as are best adapted to the narrow capacity of human understanding'. We shall not waste our time attempting to argue over things we have not the ability to argue justly about, such as the existence of God.

This leads neatly to Hume's concluding paragraphs, in which he states again the two fit areas of human enquiry, matters of fact and relations of ideas. One new feature is explained here, concerning the role of definition in the relation of ideas. It is often said that truths such as $231 - 165 = 66$ are true by definition, but nevertheless we can understand all the terms in this sum and yet the correctness or otherwise of the answer will not be obvious to us. On the other hand, if we understand 'husband' and 'wife', then the sentence 'every husband has a wife' is not only true by definition, but is transparently true. This makes it clear that not everything 'true by definition' is known in the same way.

The last paragraph of the *Enquiry* is a classic of philosophy, though somewhat hyperbolic. In it, Hume restates his 'fork' and distils the consequence of his theory for the future study of mankind. As a conclusion, it cannot be surpassed, so it is with Hume's rather than my own words that we leave this chapter:

> When we run over libraries, persuaded of these principles, what havoc must we make? If we take in our hand any volume of divinity or school metaphysics, for instance; let us ask, *Does it contain any abstract reasoning concerning quantity or number?* No. *Does it contain any experimental reasoning concerning matter of fact or existence?* No. Commit it then to the flames: for it can contain nothing but sophistry and illusion.

Summary

Hume argues that all we are directly aware of are the 'perceptions of the mind', which he divides into **ideas** and **impressions**. All ideas are copies – sometimes altered or amalgamated – of impressions, which are more or less sensations. There are three forms of connexion of ideas in the mind: Resemblance, contiguity (closeness) in time or place, and cause or effect.

Ideas and impressions are the building blocks of knowledge, which comes in two distinct forms: knowledge of **matters of fact**, which concerns what happens in the actual world; and knowledge of the **relations of ideas**, which concerns abstract reasoning of mathematics and logic, as well as things which are true by definition.

All reasoning concerning matters of fact is based on the idea of cause and effect, which in turn is explained in terms of the **necessary connexion** between the effect and its cause. But if we try and locate the impression which gives rise to this idea of necessary connexion in the world itself, we look in vain. The impression of necessary connexion is rather found within the mind itself. When we frequently observe one event to accompany or be followed by another, we are led by **custom and habit** to expect the latter when we experience the former. Hence, through habit, a necessary connexion is forged in the mind between what we call the cause and the effect. Our **inductive** reasoning, therefore, is not based on rationality but on habit.

Hume goes on to apply this general theory to several particular issues. He claims that **probability**, strictly speaking, does not exist. We say something is probable when we do not know enough about its causes to be able to predict with accuracy when it will occur, but we know from past experience what proportion of similar causes lead to the effect.

Human action is as much caused as anything else in the world, yet we do have free will. This is the **compatibilist** thesis that all freedom requires is that we act without external coercion or compulsion.

On Hume's view, we have no reason to say that animals do not reason, since they too expect future events to follow the pattern of past ones by the same non-rational mechanisms that we do.

We have no reason to suppose **miracles** ever occur, since we have more experience that tells us the laws of nature are never broken than the few testimonies which claim that they have been. Neither can we argue from the fact that the world has order to the fact that a designer God must exist, since such reasoning goes beyond the evidence of experience.

The upshot of Hume's arguments is that we should have a mitigated **scepticism**. This means accepting that there are no certain proofs for most everyday beliefs but accepting that this is just a result of inescapable limitations on human thought and no reason to doubt everything. It should, however, make us undogmatic and stop us from speculating about matters our minds are ill equipped to think about.

Glossary

Compatibilism   The view that humans have free will as long as there are no external forces making them act the way they do, even though ultimately all actions are as much subject to cause and effect as events in the natural world.

Custom and habit   The way we learn from repeated experience, rather than by logical reasoning.

Empiricism   The view that all knowledge is derived from experience, rather than from the independent operation of the intellect.

Ideas   Weaker, fainter copies of impressions. Ideas are the basic building blocks of thought and imagination.

Impressions   Sensations, feelings and emotions from which all our ideas are derived.

Induction   Reasoning from one or more particular past experiences to conclusions about the future or the general nature of the world. Such reasoning cannot proceed according to rational principles, claims Hume.

Matters of fact   Statements and beliefs about the world which are based on experience, not reason.

Miracles   Breaches of the laws of nature by divine intervention, which Hume argued we can never have reason to suppose occur.

Necessary connexion The power which links cause and effect. The existence of necessary connexion is not established by reason or by our experience of the external world.

Probability The likelihood we ascribe to an event happening when we do not know enough about its cause to be able to predict with certainty when it does or does not occur.

Rationalism The view, contrary to empiricism, which states that knowledge is acquired through the rigorous use of reason alone, without any need for the data of experience.

Relations of ideas Statements and beliefs about concepts or number, the truth of which does not depend upon fact about the actual world.

Scepticism The view that nothing can be known for certain.

Further reading

Many editions of the *Enquiry concerning Human Understanding* are available and there is little to distinguish them other than in presentation and cost. The Open Court edition, edited by Antony Flew, has some useful extra material packaged in with it, including Hume's fascinating but brief autobiographical essay.

The Enquiry concerning the Principles of Morals and the *Dialogues concerning Natural Religion* are the natural next steps for those wanting to read more Hume and are available in many editions.

A. J. Ayer's introduction to *Hume* is still a classic and is another text to be reissued as part of Oxford University Press's excellent series of *Very Short Introductions*.

Hume on Knowledge by Harold Noonan is another worthy member of the Routledge GuideBook series.

4 Bertrand Russell: *The Problems of Philosophy* (1912)

► Background

In 1912 Bertrand Russell was at the top of his profession. Volume 1 of his great work *Principia Mathematica*, written with Alfred North Whitehead, had come out two years before and the second volume was published that year. *Principia Mathematica* is an immensely difficult work and very few can claim to have really understood it all. This made it especially surprising that such an eminent philosopher should choose, at this stage of his career, to write a book intended for a popular audience. But Russell was no ordinary philosopher and *The Problems of Philosophy* became an instant classic of its kind.

The project of the *Principia* was to show how all mathematics could be deduced from a small number of self-evident logical principles. This may sound like a rather dry, uninteresting project. Viewed in the right light, however, nothing could be further from the truth.

First, philosophers have always been attracted to the possibility of setting any kind of truth on firm, unshakeable foundations. When it came to truth about reality, God, morality or our existence, this dream had come to appear more and more chimerical. Mathematics and logic were perhaps the last philosophical frontiers where such a dream could be kept alive.

Second, because logic is arguably the backbone of all philosophical reasoning, establishing its foundations had an importance for the discipline as a whole.

Third, for someone like Russell, the unchanging world of mathematics and logic was a kind of pure realm of ideas, more perfect than the changing world of people and things. Understanding the fundamental nature of this world therefore was an opportunity, in a very real sense, to have an insight into the eternal.

The *Principia* was the major work which had occupied Russell in the years before and around the writing of *The Problems of Philosophy*. It is important to bear this is mind when reading Russell, for it is easy for some parts of his work to appear dry and uninteresting. But if you understand what drew Russell to these questions, they can spring to life.

▶ **The text**

The book's title might lead you to expect a survey of Western philosophy. In fact, it is much more like an abridged and simplified account of Russell's own philosophy, with a few asides on that of others. It has been used by millions of readers as a gateway into philosophy, but it is primarily a gateway into Russell's philosophy.

The book is also a snapshot of Russell's philosophy at a particular time in his career. Russell would go on to reject many of the arguments he puts forward in *The Problems of Philosophy*. In a foreword to the 1924 German translation (included as an appendix in the current British edition) Russell lists some of the ways in which his opinions had changed. Russell lived for 46 years more after that and would come to renounce even more of the book's contents later.

However, the book is still worth reading for several reasons. First of all, in most cases, the reasons for Russell's later rejections of some ideas in *The Problems of Philosophy* are extremely complex and one stands no chance of understanding them unless one first gets to grips with what it is that is being rejected. Second, the book shows the Russellian system of philosophy at its apotheosis. Over time, its key tenets would come under increased attack. This is a chance to get a glimpse of his theories in their boldest and most confident guise. It is often most instructive to read the works which stand as monuments to an intellectual movement's peak, even if it is downhill from then on. We see Russell's system in its fullest glory here, before sustained attack begins to tarnish it.

But perhaps the main reason to read the book is that it is an incredibly lucid example of the best of early twentieth-century British philosophy. Some look back at this period and see the work that was done as tedious, narrow and obsessed with boring considerations about language. In Russell we have someone who, while representing the concerns of that generation of philosophers, was never narrow, dry or boring. *The Problems of Philosophy* is thus an invaluable entry point to what can be an intimidating and bewildering chapter in Western philosophy's history.

▶ **1 Appearance and reality**

Russell's first question echoes the one Descartes addressed in his *Meditations*: 'Is there any knowledge in the world which is so certain that no reasonable man could doubt it?' Also in an echo of Descartes, he answers this by turning to everyday objects to show just how much of our knowledge is dubitable.

Russell observes that, although we usually have a clear idea of what a thing is *really* like, we rarely perceive it as we think it really is. For example, the 'real' colour of a table might be black all over, but when we see a table, the reflections of light mean that the table does not appear to have a uniform colour. Similarly, the effect of perspective is to distort the 'real' shape of objects. So none of the perceptions we have reveal directly the true properties of objects. Rather, we infer from our perceptions what the true properties of objects are, and we suppose that it is these true properties which are the *cause* of what we perceive. This is a basic version of what has come to be known as 'the causal theory of perception'.

Several questions are raised by this explanation. First, on what grounds can we conclude which are the real properties of an object? For example, given that colours appear different under different lighting conditions, why should the colour under standard conditions be considered the 'real' colour? Second, if we never perceive the object itself directly, how can we really say what the object itself is like? Third, is there such a thing as the 'real' object at all? These questions are taken up later by Russell.

One very important aspect of Russell's argument is that what we directly perceive are not objects themselves, but perceptions, or 'sense data' (singular: sense datum). The belief that there are sense data is often argued for along these lines:

1 I do not directly perceive the table.
2 I do directly perceive something.
3 What I directly perceive is therefore not an object, but rather a perception, which can be called a 'sense datum'.

It can also be defended on the following grounds, usually called the argument from illusion:

1 The same stick can appear bent (when in water) or straight.
2 It cannot be both bent and straight.
3 As the stick is not bent when I see it in water, it cannot be the stick I am seeing.
4 Therefore, I must be seeing something else, which can be called a 'sense datum'.

This argument concludes that we see sense data when we see an object not as it is. But given that all experiences of a given sense (sight, touch and so on) are of the same general character, it seems to make more sense to say that we always perceive sense data than that we sometimes see an object and sometimes see sense data.

The sense data theory has been extremely influential, but J. L. Austin in his *Sense and Sensibilia* rejected it on three grounds.

First, Austin rejected the argument from illusion on the grounds that 'familiarity takes the edge off illusion'. To say that we are often the victims of illusions is a nonsense. A coin viewed from the side must appear elliptical, for that is the only way a coin so viewed can appear in our world. We would expect a stick to appear bent in water, unless we are very young children. The point is that we are not presented with all these inaccurate representations of ordinary objects. Rather, we see objects just as they should appear. So the idea that I cannot be seeing the object if that object looks bent or a different shape is absurd.

The second mistake Austin claimed sense data theorists make is to conclude that the appearance something has is some kind of *thing*, that is a sense datum. It is rather a kind of property of the thing. For example, when I see a stick that looks bent, I am not seeing a thing which is not the stick. Rather, I am seeing the stick which, because of its position, appears bent. There is simply no reason to suppose that another thing, a sense datum, comes between me and the object. This is the mistake of 'reification' – thinking of a phenomenon which is not an object as though it were an object.

Austin also thought the sense data theorist was wrong to say that we perceive objects indirectly. If this is true, it must make sense to ask what perceiving directly would entail. But however we or any being perceived, it would always have to be through some sense (as that is what perception means) and it will usually be through some medium, be it a gas, liquid or solid. In any such case, there will be an object, senses and a medium, each of which will contribute something to the character of the perception. Hence, it is not clear what our current perceptions lack which direct perceptions would contain. In short, the direct/indirect distinction is in this context empty.

Austin's objections together shed some doubt on the distinction Russell draws between appearance and reality and on the sustainability of the sense data theory in general.

▶ 2 The existence of matter

Is there such a thing as matter?

Russell has argued that what we immediately perceive are simply sense data. Common sense tells us that these sense data correspond to really existing physical objects that are independent of these sense data. In other words, there is a permanent reality behind the 'veil of appearances'. This permanent reality is made up of matter – sense-independent 'stuff'.

However, it is logically possible that there is no such thing as matter. Perhaps all that exists is *you*, and that what you see, hear and touch are simply parts of your own mind, and that there is no external world at all. As in dreams, although what you see appears to have independent reality, there is in fact nothing to the things you perceive other than the perceptions themselves.

This scepticism may run even deeper. Although Descartes might have been right to argue 'I think, therefore I am', this doesn't tell us very much about the nature of this 'I'. The 'I' that reads this paragraph may well not be the same 'I' that read the last one. Indeed, there may not have been an 'I' that read the last paragraph: maybe, as in dreams again, I seem to remember reading it when in fact, I didn't.

So the problem is this: We have to grant that (i) there are such things as sense data and (ii) there must be someone perceiving these sense data. But can we go further than this and conclude that (iii) the sense data correspond to physically existing objects and (iv) that the 'I' that thinks is a persisting entity?

One attempted solution is to say that, although it is true that ten people sitting around a table do not see exactly the same thing, they can agree on enough for us to be convinced that the table does have more or less consistent properties. The differences in our sense data can be accounted for by the different perspectives we occupy. But this is a poor solution, because until we are sure that the external world is really out there, we cannot be sure that other people aren't also merely sense data. If Joe Bloggs tells you the table is white, all that shows is that you have a certain series of sense data of a person talking. But as that doesn't show the sense data correspond to an actual person and actual words, so his testimony cannot be evidence for the existence of an external world. If everyone in your dream agrees that the sky is green, it doesn't mean that there is a green sky that exists independently of your dream.

The way to resolve this problem is much simpler. At the moment there are two possibilities: (i) All that exist are sense data. (ii) There exist both sense data and matter. Both are logically possible. But although the second postulates the existence of more entities (sense data and matter rather than just the former), it is still by far the most economical explanation. For example, the movements and behaviour of my cat are puzzling if she only exists as sense data. In this world, she keeps popping in and out of existence, depending on whether I see her or not. What is more, she gets hungry at the same rate, whether she exists or not! With other people, it is even more puzzling if they do not exist unless as sense data. So the solution is really simple: the hypothesis that things really do exist, independently of my perceptions, has more explanatory power than the thesis that they do not. We can account for so much more if we suppose the existence of matter than if we deny it.

Unlike Descartes, who attempts to build up knowledge from indubitable foundations, Russell works in a more 'holistic' way. He examines our various instinctive beliefs and sees whether or not there is room to doubt them or not. But he doesn't use immunity from doubt as a criterion for sound beliefs. Rather, where there is doubt, we have to ask whether those doubtable beliefs fit in with our other beliefs in a way which is consistent.

In this way, Russell sees the function of philosophy as more modest than, say, Descartes, who thought we could achieve through philosophy firm and ultimate knowledge of all of reality.

▶ 3 The nature of matter

Russell has already argued that, although reality and appearance are different, things do exist independently of our perceptions of them, and thus there is such a thing as matter. He now turns to consider what we can know about this matter.

Part of the answer to this question comes from science. Matter is, in essence, motion. Matter may have other properties, but whatever these other properties are, they do not help us to understand what matter is. It has to be understood, however, that what we perceive is not motion. For example, it is incorrect to say 'light is a form of wave-motion'. Rather we should say, 'wave-motion is the *cause* of light', as 'light' is that which we directly observe through our senses, whereas wave-motion is not perceived at all. A congenitally blind person can never know what light is, but he may understand what wave-motion is as well as we can. This shows that light is something essentially to do with our perceptions, whereas wave-motion is not.

Similar things may also be said about sounds, tastes, smells and tactile sensations. But what about space and time? Surely these belong to the real world as surely as they belong to our perceptions? Russell answers yes and no. We can follow his stages of thought thus: (1) Space is not really as it appears to us. Round objects appear elliptical, and so on. (2) However, the shape we perceive is connected to its real shape. We can say that its real shape is the *cause* of how the shape appears to us. (3) For this to be possible, there must be a real space which my body and the objects I perceive is in. (4) The positions of real objects in this space must be more or less as I perceive them. Were they not, I would find myself bumping into things that look far away, or it taking longer to reach a near building than a distant one, for example.

So far, so good. But though there is this correspondence between our *perceptions* of time and space and *real* time and space, all we can know about this real time and space is 'what is required to secure the correspondence'. What Russell means by this is that the ordering of physical objects is known to us, but the precise nature of the space in which they are ordered cannot be known by us. Similarly with time: we may know that one event comes before or after another, but as to whether objective time passes, how fast it passes and so on, we cannot know. The real world is thus ordered as we perceive it, but this is all we know and, indeed, need to know in order for there to be a general correspondence between our perceptions and the real world.

Note, however, that some events may *superficially* appear to be ordered other than as they really are, such as thunder and lightning, which though simultaneous, often appear to occur at two different times.

Other qualities can also be understood in this relative way. Two blue objects can be supposed to have some corresponding similarity, and two differently coloured objects some corresponding difference. But we have no hope of being directly acquainted with the real cause of these differences and similarities.

Some would argue that physical objects are more or less like the sense data we have of them. Such an idea is not definitely refutable, but is groundless none the less. All sense data are the result of a process which involves our senses, the objects and the intervening environment. To suppose that the end products, the sense data, resemble the object itself, is rather far fetched, as it would require a similarity between object and perception quite unnecessary for the process of perception. If there were a similarity, it would appear to be quite a remarkable coincidence.

In conclusion, the nature of matter must remain somewhat mysterious. We have good reasons for believing it to be there, and for there to be a correspondence between what we perceive and what is there. But given that this correspondence requires only relative similarities, such as a sameness of ordering, to suppose any greater similarity is to suppose more than can be justified.

▶ 4 Idealism

Idealism is the view that whatever exists (or can be known to exist) is in some sense mental.

Although this seems absurd, remember that Russell has already concluded that if physical objects exist, they are different from the sense data we perceive, so the truth about physical objects must be strange, and may be unattainable.

One of the most famous idealists, George Berkeley, argued for idealism along these lines:

1 Sense data (or 'ideas') cannot exist independently of us (i.e. thinking beings).
2 Ideas exist in the mind.
3 The only things we know are sense data.
4 Therefore, to be known is to be in the mind.
5 Therefore, everything that can be known must be in the mind (i.e. it must be mental).
6 As we have no reason to suppose that what cannot be known exists, all that exists is therefore mental.

A concrete example may help to show what Berkeley was getting at. When we see a tree, all we actually see are 'ideas' of shape, colour, texture and so on. Although common sense tells us trees exist independently of us, since all we ever perceive are ideas of the tree, Berkeley believes there are no grounds for this common-sense belief. For every object, its being consists in it being perceived: its *esse* is *percipi*. Berkeley devised a test to prove this: Try and think of anything that is not an idea. As soon as you think of it, you already defeat your purpose, because in thinking of it, it becomes an idea. And even though there are things which you may never think of, unless someone could think of them, there is no sense in saying that they exist. A thing which cannot be an idea is nothing at all. Hence, the only things that exist are ideas.

Russell believes there are several mistakes which arguments for idealism make. First, idealism moves from the thought that ideas are in the mind, to the thought that any object is only a set of ideas, to the idea that objects are in the mind. But when we consider what 'in the mind' means, this deduction becomes suspect. If I have someone 'in mind', that doesn't mean that person is actually in my head, it just means that the idea of that person is in my head. So in order to know an object, it is not necessary for the object to be in my head, it is only necessary for the thought of the object to be in my head. Berkeley believed that as we only know an object by the ideas we have of the object, the object must only be an idea. Russell's argument shows that this needn't be the case at all (though his argument isn't enough to show it isn't the case).

Second, Berkeley believes he has shown that if something is known, it must be mental. But this doesn't follow at all. We need to distinguish between two things: the thing we are aware of and the awareness itself. Whilst it is clear that *awareness* must be mental, what we are *aware of* need not be. Berkeley seems to be conflating the act of perception with the object perceived.

This act/object distinction is important. It is characteristic of the mind that it can be aware of things other than itself. So to say 'things known must be in the mind' would seem to deny this basic feature of minds. Either that, or it means 'things known must be before the mind', but that is just a tautology which allows for the possibility that the thing before the mind is not mental. Again, Russell has not shown that idealism must be false, but he has shown that the most common reasons given for believing idealism are not good ones.

▶ 5 Acquaintance and description

In this chapter, Russell distinguishes between knowledge by description and knowledge by acquaintance.

We have knowledge by acquaintance of those things which we are directly aware of. In addition to sense data these also include:

Memories These do not give us knowledge by acquaintance of the past, but merely of our recollections of the past.

Introspection This is acquaintance with the contents of our own minds, which is sometimes called 'second-order knowledge'. For example, we and animals have an awareness of external objects. But only we, and possibly other 'higher' animals, can introspect and be aware of our awareness. In this way, 'my awareness of the sun' is something which I can be directly aware of.

Ourselves? Russell isn't sure on this one. Russell believes that if we can be acquainted though introspection with such things as 'my feeling hungry', then we must be acquainted with two different things: (i) my hunger and (ii) that which feels this hunger. If we were not acquainted with (ii), then our awareness of our hunger would lack the second-order properties he has already argued it can have. However, although this implies awareness of a self, it doesn't necessitate an awareness of a permanent or continuing self. Therefore, the extent to which we are aware of what we normally think a self to be is debatable.

Universals General ideas are also known by acquaintance. Russell talks more about universals in Chapters 9 and 10.

When we talk about knowledge by description, we should note that there are two types of description: definite and ambiguous (or indefinite) descriptions. An indefinite description is *a so and so*, and a definite description is *the so and so*. An object known by description is always known by a definite description. If it were not, we could not tell which object we were talking about, so it could hardly be known!

We have *mere* knowledge by description when we cannot say 'X is the so and so', where X is a proper noun or a demonstrative pronoun such as 'that' or 'this'. For example, we know by description 'the tallest man in the world', but unless we know who this person is, so that we can say 'X is the strongest man in the world', we know this man merely by description.

Now to the real 'meat' of Russell's theory. Given that we only know by acquaintance the things listed above, it is clear that we cannot know objects in themselves, or indeed other people by acquaintance. Therefore, we can only know them by description. So when we use proper nouns such as 'Max Bygraves', these names are really a kind of shorthand for descriptions. In other words: 'The thought of a person using a proper name correctly can only be expressed explicitly if we replace the proper name by a description.'

It is clear that the description we would replace the proper name with will vary from person to person (and indeed from time to time). For some, Max Bygraves is 'that very talented and warm entertainer', whilst for others with less taste, he is 'that old codger on British TV'. However, just so long as the object the name refers to is the same, the truth or falsehood of sentences containing that proper name is unaffected by which description the name would be replaced with.

These descriptions will be found to consist solely of one or more particulars with which we are acquainted, and universals. In the case of historical figures, there will be universals such as 'queen' or 'man' and particulars which we have received through written or spoken testimony. With people we know, the descriptions will consist mostly of particulars with which we are acquainted, all of which are basically sense data. But in both cases, the general principle holds that 'every proposition which we can understand must be composed wholly of constituents with which we are acquainted'. The model is like this:

Acquaintance	Descriptions	Proper nouns
Sense data, universals, etc. *e.g. tall, man, etc.*	A so and so or the so and so *e.g. The tall man next door*	Shorthand for descriptions *e.g. Mr Jones*

In other words, proper nouns are really descriptions and all descriptions consist of elements known by acquaintance. It is knowledge by acquaintance which is the foundation of all knowledge, but it is knowledge by description which enables us to 'pass beyond the limits of our private experience'.

Of course, when we use names, we intend to refer to the person or thing itself. But that, argues Russell, we cannot do, as we are not acquainted with the thing itself. But because we can describe the thing itself, we can talk about it.

Russell's theory entails that though what we mean by our sentences varies (because the descriptions we would replace proper nouns with vary from person to person), we can still talk about the same things because what our descriptions refer to are the same. But in some ways, Russell leaves how this is the case mysterious. The meanings of all propositions should be traced back to particulars and universals with which we are acquainted, and all of these things are private to ourselves. The question therefore remains, how do we get from private acquaintance to public description? Once more this seems like a problem of the sense data theory. Because we are only aware of our private sense data, it is hard to see how we can get beyond our own experience to the public domain. Russell's response would have to be his previous arguments supporting the existence of an external world which more or less corresponds to our sense data, and of the existence of other minds. This belief might be enough to make it reasonable to suppose that what I am describing is the same as what you are describing when we talk about someone like Max Bygraves.

▶ 6 Induction

How can we reason from what we know by acquaintance to knowledge of other people, the past, real objects and so on?

It is important to consider this chapter in the light of what has preceded it. Russell has already tried to dispel scepticism concerning the real existence of matter. So he is not here concerned solely with justifying our beliefs about the world, but also with trying to find out what the principle is which enables us to makes these inferences. However, there is one important difference between this and the earlier discussion. Before, Russell discussed how the existence of sense data justified belief in the existence of external objects. Now, he is concerned with how the existence of one sort of thing can be taken as a sign of the existence of another sort of thing.

A typical question this concerns is whether the sun will rise tomorrow. We know it has done so every day for billions of years, but why should it do so tomorrow? Well, the laws of motion say it will. But again, though the laws of motion have held for a long time, why should they continue to hold tomorrow? It is clear that we needn't be concerned to show they *must* hold tomorrow, only that it is extremely *probable* that they will.

Frequent repetition of a uniform succession (e.g. night following day) or coexistence (e.g. thunder and lightning) is often the *cause* of our expectation that the succession or coexistence will happen again. But this doesn't *justify* our expectation, as these expectations are prone to be misleading, as is the case with the hapless turkey who, expecting to be fed when the sun rises, has its neck wrung on Christmas Eve.

The basic belief we are looking to justify is in the uniformity of nature. This is the belief that everything that happens is an instance of a general law to which there are no exceptions. If we find a true exception to a law we have formulated, then it is an assumption of science that there is another more basic law which explains this, and that this law is exceptionless. It must be remembered that the laws of science hold and exist whether we have a good grasp of them or not. So far, our belief in the uniformity of nature has been vindicated. But can we rely on it being vindicated in the future?

One answer is that, in the past there was a future, and we believed it would be like the past, and it was. Therefore, we already have evidence that the future is like the past. But this is a bad answer, as though we have experience of *past futures*, we have not had experience of *future futures*. So the question remains, only in a different form: will future futures resemble past futures?

The principle we need is the principle of induction. In essence this principle states that if two things are found to be associated with each other and never found disassociated from each other, then the more cases we have of them associated, the greater is the probability that they will continue to be associated in the future. This holds for particular associations and general laws.

A few things need to be noted about this principle. First, it concerns probability, so counter-examples do not disprove it. It is improbable that I should win the lottery, and if I do win it, it doesn't show I was wrong to think it improbable. Similarly, if an inductive inference leads to a conclusion that turns out to be false (for example, 'all swans are white'), that in itself doesn't show my inference was a bad one.

Second, induction should not be crude. If we know, for example, that human behaviour or colours are prone to be variable, then we should be careful about making generalised inferences about either of them. This is why the turkey's inference and the inference about swans are poor ones.

If you are not convinced by the principle, Russell has a stern warning: 'We must either accept the inductive principle or forgo all justification of our expectations about the future. All our conduct depends on accepting it.' (Note the similarities to Hume – see Chapter 3 on the *Enquiry concerning Human Understanding*.) However, it is not clear that this really justifies the principle.

One problem with this principle is that we don't always need many cases to make an inductive inference: one bite is often enough to make us shy! Also, continued association is not always grounds for an inductive inference. The stunt person who has always survived unscathed cannot be confident that this will continue. This shows how Russell seems mistaken to put so much stress on sheer *number* of associations. It seems the *type* of association is just as important, if not more so, and on this subject he is silent.

In summary, Russell seems to leave us in the same boat as the turkey, but just a little bit shrewder!

▶ 7 Knowledge of general principles

The principle of induction is not the only principle which cannot be proved or disproved by experience, but which none the less we are certain of. Such principles are often used in arguments which start from experience, drawing inferences from what is given in sensation. They are often so obvious we don't even realise we are using them. But we do. They are general principles, which Russell goes on to explain.

How do we get these principles? There is usually a three-stage process we go through: (1) We recognise a particular principle. (2) We realise the particular details are irrelevant. (3) We form general principles. As one example, take maths: (1) We notice that two cars added to two other cars makes four cars. (2) We realise that it needn't be cars we are talking about. (3) We form the general principle that $2 + 2 = 4$.

Consider another example from logic:

1 If yesterday was the 15th, today is the 16th.
2 Yesterday was the 15th.
3 Therefore, today is the 16th.

This form of argument can be used whatever we are talking about. The general form of this argument is:

1	If this is true, that is true.	1	If X, then Y.
2	This is true.	2	X.
3	That is true.	3	Y.

This is one instance of a yet more general principle, which is involved in all logical demonstrations: 'Anything implied by a true proposition is true.'

There are more such principles, the most basic being:

The Law of Identity 'Whatever is, is.'
The Law of Contradiction 'Nothing can both be and not be.'
The Law of the Excluded Middle 'Everything must either be or not be.'

These are often called laws of thought, but it should be noted that they don't just govern how we should think. It is believed that if we follow these rules, we think properly. Therefore, the laws apply to the world and not just to our own thoughts.

How do we get these principles? Empiricists claim that all knowledge is gained through experience, including knowledge of these principles. Rationalists believe that some knowledge is innate, although it is perhaps better to say *a priori*, meaning that it cannot be proved or demonstrated by experience, even though we may need experience to elicit and cause this knowledge. Russell believes that though the empiricists were right to say that experience is needed if we are to know these principles, the rationalists were correct in their more fundamental claim that these laws cannot be proved or disproved by experience.

We also acquire these principles differently to how we acquire empirical knowledge. The certainty of empirical knowledge increases the more experiences confirm the empirical hypothesis we believe, though it is always logically possible that empirical truths are false. But to know an *a priori* general principle we only need one experience from which we can generalise, and it is logically impossible that such a principle is false. For example, considering just one example can show us that two plus two must always equal four, whereas thousands of experiences of the sun rising can only show us that it is highly probable that the sun will rise tomorrow.

One other respect in which the empiricists were right is that existence cannot be proved *a priori*. This is because all *a priori* knowledge is, in effect, hypothetical, of the form 'if X, then Y'. Although we know *a priori* that anything implied by a true proposition is true, we cannot know if the original proposition is true except through experience. This is one reason why Descartes's proofs for the existence of

God fail. Descartes can show that existence is part of the essence of God, but this doesn't show that there is a God which would then have this essence. In effect, Descartes shows that if God exists, he exists! (see Chapter 2 on the *Meditations*).

Ethical principles are also *a priori*. Experience cannot prove that the greatest happiness principle is true, or that murder is wrong. Maths and geometry are also known *a priori*.

The differences between induction and deduction can now be clearly seen. Deductive arguments go from the general to the general or from the general to the particular. Induction argues from the particular to the particular or from the particular to the general. It would thus appear that induction is most suited to empirical generalisations about the world. This is because deductions require general principles, which in empirical cases are no more than probable and are always less certain than particular generalisations (see the section above on induction). So when constructing an argument about the empirical world, rather than using induction to get a merely probable general principle and then make a deduction from that, it is far less roundabout to stick to induction in the first place.

▶ 8　How is *a priori* knowledge possible?

This chapter in *The Problems of Philosophy* is really Russell's discussion of Kant's answer to this question. Kant is difficult, but the real key to understanding him is to focus on the terms and concepts he uses. But note that Kant doesn't always use concepts in the standard way.

Kant is credited with inventing 'critical philosophy', where it is taken as a datum (or given) that we have knowledge, and we then deduce conclusions from this fact. This is also known as using transcendental arguments.

Previous to Kant, all *a priori* knowledge was taken to be analytic, that is to say, any predicate (roughly, a property or description of something) we deduce about a subject (the thing the predicate describes) must already be in the subject. For example, with 'a bald man is bald', the predicate 'bald' is contained in the subject 'bald man'. Maths was also supposed to operate along these lines: in '7 + 5 = 12', '12' is taken to be wholly contained within '7 + 5'. So the law of contradiction is all we need to establish the truth of *a priori* knowledge, as it would be contradictory to claim that any predicate of an *a priori* judgement was false if it were contained in the subject.

Hume launched the first salvo against the orthodox view when he claimed that knowledge of the principle of cause and effect was not *a priori* (see Chapter 3 on *An Enquiry concerning Human Understanding*.) This implied a scepticism which troubled Kant. Kant's way out was to challenge the way in which knowledge is divided up. Kant argued that it was possible to have *a priori* knowledge which was synthetic, not analytic (in other words, where the predicate does add something to the subject). His simplest example was '7 + 5 = 12'. Although clearly *a priori* – as though true, it cannot be proved or disproved by experience – Kant claimed it was *not* an analytic statement. '12', he claimed, is not contained within '7 + 5'. It is a new idea. This is shown by the fact that someone can have the ideas of '7', ' + ' and '5' and yet not have the idea of '12'. A child who can only count and add up to ten is one such example.

Kant's next question was, how is this knowledge then possible? If the idea deduced *a priori* is new, where did it come from? Certainly not from experience, as all experience is particular, yet *a priori* knowledge is general.

Kant's solution was his famous Copernican revolution. Copernicus had shifted the centre of our view of the universe from the Earth to the sun. Kant's shift was from objects to ourselves. He claimed that, rather than our knowledge conforming to objects, objects must conform to our knowledge. This goes back to what critical philosophy means. We have knowledge. How is this possible? Because there is a certain form to which all experience must conform. This form is of space and time, and also contains *a priori* principles such as the law of contradiction. We can only have experiences if objects conform to the dictates of space, time and such principles. Thus space and time are features, not of the world, but of our nature. Secondary qualities are, however, caused by objects themselves. This is shown by the fact that colour, texture and so on are not necessary for our experience. They are rather things added as a result of our interaction with the objects themselves. However, the true nature of these objects must remain unknown. We must confine our knowledge to phenomena (appearances) and remain ignorant of noumena (things in themselves). The certainty of our *a priori* knowledge is thus guaranteed by the fact that it is knowledge of the way we necessarily experience the world, and not knowledge of the way the world actually is.

Russell claims that the basic flaw of Kant's position is that if it is our nature which is the basis of *a priori* knowledge, how can it be at all certain? Could not our nature change? Returning to an earlier theme, it makes *a priori* knowledge governed by laws *merely* of thought, rather than rules which, if followed, guarantee that our thoughts are true. Kant's reply would be that Russell hasn't grasped how important our nature is for us to have any experience of the world at all. Either we have experiences in space and time which conform to certain *a priori* principles or we have no experience or knowledge at all.

As I warned, Kant is tricky to get to grips with, but it is worth spending some time making the effort with him, since his influence has been enormous in philosophy.

▶ 9 The world of universals

Russell's collaborator on his magnum opus, *Principia Mathematica*, Alfred North Whitehead, famously said that 'the safest general characterisation of the European philosophical tradition is that it consists of a series of footnotes to Plato.' As if to illustrate Whitehead's point, Russell now turns to talk about universals, acknowledging that the theory he is describing is 'largely Plato's, with merely such modifications as time has shown to be necessary'.

Plato's theory was the theory of forms and the problem it deals with is that of universals. Universals contrast with particulars. For example, there are many particular cows that exist, but there is also a universal – 'cow' – which is not any one particular cow. We use universals all the time and don't find them puzzling. But if you think about it, universals have an odd status. A cow is a real animal in the real world; but what is 'cow'? It is some kind of concept or idea that exists independently of any particular cow. When you start to think about universals in this way, they can appear to be mysterious, ethereal entities.

Plato's theory of the forms explains universals by saying that, in the case of cows, for example, there is a common nature or essence which all particular cows share in. It is because they all somehow partake of this 'form of the cow' that they are individual cows. What is more, whereas particular cows can be turned into burgers at any moment, the pure form of 'cowness' is eternal and indestructible. Even if all the cows in the world are wiped out, the form of the cow continues to exist as a kind of pure idea.

But what exactly are these forms? Are they strange non-physical entities as Plato sometimes seemed to suggest? Or are they just ideas in our minds? Russell sidesteps this debate as he is more concerned to look at how universals function in our language and logic than to delve into their ontological status. (This is perhaps indicative of twentieth-century British philosophy's preference for issues of language and logic over questions about metaphysics and existence.)

Russell contends that every sentence contains at least one universal. This is not surprising because only proper nouns – words that name particular individuals – are *not* universals. 'Daisy is a lovely cow', for example, only contains one particular – Daisy. All the other words are universals because they refer not to particular, but to general concepts: being ('is'), loveliness, and cow. (It is not clear that 'a' *refers* to anything, but it certainly does not refer to a particular). If all sentences contain universals and all truths are sentences or propositions, it follows that 'all knowledge of truths involves acquaintance with universals'.

But although universals are so prevalent and important, Russell believes that philosophy has failed by not paying enough attention to them. Philosophers have focused on substantive universals (nouns such as justice, person and square) and adjectives (such as true, green or mortal). But they have tended to neglect verbs (such as know, live and see) and propositions (such as on, in and towards). This bias has led philosophers to concentrate on things and their properties rather than the relations between things. This is a serious omission, because one can only truly understand the way the world is if one attends to the relations between things as well as to the individual things themselves.

Russell considers as an example the relation 'north of', with the example of 'Edinburgh is north of London'. Russell's main aim here is to show that such a relation is real in the world and not merely something in our own minds. But although it is real, it is not like most things in the world, which can be observed by the senses or through introspection.

Russell was always attracted by the idea of truths which are somehow immortal and beyond change. At the end of this chapter, he talks about the world of universals belonging to the world of being, which is 'unchangeable, rigid, exact, delightful to the mathematician . . . '. He contrasts this with the world of existence, which he calls 'fleeting, vague, without sharp boundaries'. This reflects a certain kind of mind which is attracted to mathematics and logic because it sees something beautiful, perhaps even sublime, in its certainty and unchangeability.

What Russell doesn't mention is Aristotle's famous 'third man' argument against the theory of forms. The forms are postulated by Plato to explain how two particular things, say, two cows, can both be cows. The answer is that they share a similarity with a third thing, the form of the cow. But, asks Aristotle, if we need a third thing, the form of the cow, to account for the resemblance between both cows, how do we account for the fact that each cow resembles the form of the cow? Surely we need to say here that the cow resembles the form of the cow because there is a third thing, call it the 'form of the form of the cow', which has the features in common between the cow and the form of the cow? If we allow this, before very long we start off on an infinite regress, postulating forms of forms of forms of cows *ad infinitum*.

The problem, argued Aristotle, is that you do not need to postulate the existence of a third thing to explain the similarity between two things. Not only do you not need this third thing, it is disastrous if you think you do. For if similarity between two things always requires a third thing, then there is no end to the number of 'third' things you need to postulate, as is shown by the need for a form of the form of the form of the cow.

Russell doesn't deal with this objection. He simply moves on in the next chapter to the question of our knowledge of universals.

▶ 10 Our knowledge of universals

Russell was a prodigious writer and in many of his popular works, of which *The Problems of Philosophy* is one, we are often presented with what appears to be Russell's train of thought directly transcribed. This means some texts can meander. This chapter has something of this quality and as a result is a jumble of related points and arguments rather than a clear, linear discussion.

In Chapter 5 Russell argued that knowledge is divided between that which we have from acquaintance and that which we have from description. Knowledge of universals is no exception to this.

Universals we know from acquaintance include those known through sense experience: colours, tastes, sounds, smells and textures. We know what white is, for example, because we experience many different patches of white and abstract from that the universal 'white' of which all these particular patches of white partake.

Time-relations and space-relations are also known by acquaintance. It is experience that teaches us that X is to the left of Y, or that this happened before that. In this way, relations such as 'to the left of' or 'before' are known by acquaintance. Resemblance and similarity are also known by acquaintance.

We might now expect Russell to list those universals we know by description. In fact, he finds himself arguing for the main thesis of this chapter, namely that 'all *a priori* knowledge deals exclusively with the relations of universals'.

Russell seems to assume that it is obvious why this might be presumed to be true. If we consider some examples of *a priori* propositions, it does indeed seem to be the case that they deal only with universals. 'All bachelors are unmarried men', for example, deals only with universals. A similar proposition which included a particular, such as 'Johnny is a bachelor', would not be *a priori*, since we could only know it to be true if we knew some facts about Johnny's marital status. Similarly, mathematical truths are also *a priori*: '2 + 2 = 4' is a proposition about abstract numbers, not about things.

However, Russell identifies a potential counter-example. Some apparently universal statements could be interpreted as saying something about a class of particulars. For instance, '2 + 2 = 4' could be interpreted as meaning 'any collection formed of two twos is a collection of four'. If this were the case, then '2 + 2 = 4', though an *a priori* proposition, would be as much about particular collections of twos and fours as it would be about universals. So to defend his claim that all *a priori* knowledge deals *exclusively* with universals, he has to show that '2 + 2 = 4' is not a proposition about particular collections of twos and fours.

Russell's response to this challenge is swift and incisive. His basic point is that what we need to know to understand '2 + 2 = 4' are truths about universals, not particulars. Although it may be true that, once we have understood what it means, we can see that it implies truths about particular pairs and sets of four, the proposition is not about such sets. Consider this parallel. The truth 'only UK citizens can be knighted by the queen' implies something about Chinese citizens – namely that they cannot be knighted. But it is clearly not a statement *about* Chinese citizens. Similarly, mathematical truths have implications for actual sets of things, but they are not about such sets.

What is more, the translation from universals to particulars is not direct anyway. Consider 1 + 1 = 2. We only know that one person plus another person leaves us with two people because we are familiar with people and how they work. It does not follow as a matter of *a priori* logic. If you are unconvinced, consider what happens when you add one drop of water to another drop of water. You don't get two drops of water, but one larger drop! So although it sometimes seems that our knowledge of *a priori* truths allows us to know in advance some truths about particulars, in fact, all knowledge of particulars depends on our experience of their nature.

Russell now finds himself off the subject of universals *per se*, considering some of the interesting features of general *a priori* propositions. One of the most remarkable of these is that we can know something is the case without knowing a single instance of it. To give one of Russell's examples in simpler language, 'all the numbers which are the product of adding together two other numbers and which have never been thought of by any human being are over 100.' We can know this to be true even though we cannot give a single example of such a number (since as soon as we do so, the number has been thought of by a human being).

Russell is led by his discussion back to his division between knowledge by acquaintance and knowledge by description. Truths we know by acquaintance can be called *self-evident* truths and we know these to be true *intuitively*. These include basic truths of mathematics and logic and what is given to us in sense experience. Interestingly, Russell also suggests some moral truths may belong to this category, but this is not a view he persisted in holding. From these self-evident truths, we can discover *derivative* truths using deduction. This concept of intuitive knowledge is important and is the subject of his next chapter.

But first, it is worth noting some remarks Russell makes about sense data. Russell says, '. . . whatever may be the object of acquaintance, even in dreams and hallucinations, there is no error involved so long as we don't go beyond the immediate object'. For example, if I think I see an elephant, there may or may not be an elephant present. But I cannot be wrong that I had the experience of seeing an elephant.

However, this view came to be criticised more and more in later years. The problem is that an experience itself does not seem to be true or false: it is just had. Therefore, it seems odd to say we cannot be in error about our experiences, since we cannot be right about them either. We can only be right or wrong if we say something *about* an experience. This is a point Russell acknowledges in the next chapter. But now, it is not obvious that 'I seemed to see an elephant' *is* indubitably true if I think it is. For example, I may misunderstand the word 'elephant', and what I thought I saw was really hippopotamus-like. The problem is that language is a public medium and has public rules for its correct use. So there seems to be no way in which I can guarantee that any proposition describing my own experience is correct since I cannot guarantee I am using language correctly.

▶ 11 On intuitive knowledge

People often complain of philosophers that they are forever demanding proofs or demonstrations which the real world cannot provide. You can't prove everything. As it happens, Russell (along with almost all other philosophers) agrees. There are limits to proof and this chapter on intuitive knowledge explains one of the most important of these.

If you ask for a justification or proof for anything, that justification or proof will itself depend upon some further truth being accepted. For example, if I demonstrate to you that water is H_2O by a laboratory experiment, my demonstration only stands if you accept some other truths about all water being basically the same, or the soundness of my experimental techniques. We could, in turn, demonstrate these things by further experiments and tests. But eventually, our proofs and demonstrations have to end with the acceptance of certain basic truths which do not in themselves require further justification. Some things we just have to accept as true.

This isn't generally a problem, because these basic truths are so simple as to be self-evident. They include basic mathematical truths, such as '1 + 1 = 2', and basic logical truths, such as 'something cannot be and not be at the same time'. From these basic, self-evident truths, we can demonstrate more complex ones. (An interesting historical note here is that Russell confidently asserts: 'All arithmetic, moreover, can be deduced from the general principles of logic.' This was the main thesis of his and Whitehead's *Principia Mathematica*. However, Wittgenstein and Gödel both independently showed this to be demonstrably false.)

Russell notes that these self-evident general principles are harder to grasp than particular self-evident truths. It is easy for people to see that 'it can't be Monday and not Monday at the same time', for example, but it is harder to grasp the truth and meaning of 'something cannot be and not be at the same time'. This requires practice in abstract thought.

Russell also talks about intuitive judgements of sense, which we discussed at the end of the last section. He adds to this another type of intuitive knowledge, that given by memory. As Russell readily admits, memory is tricky because we so often remember things incorrectly. So why does he include it as a class of intuitive knowledge when the other members of this class are self-evidently and transparently true? He does this by saying that 'self-evidence has degrees'. Basic truths of logic and perception have a high degree of self-evidence while more complex mathematics and logic are less self-evident. The extent to which memories are self-evidently true depends upon how recent the events remembered are.

This is not very satisfactory, however. Psychological research into memory shows that it is a very unreliable guide to truth. It is hard to see how anyone fully aware of the tricks memory plays could ever see memory as being a source of self-evident knowledge.

Russell is perhaps aware of this, since he ends the chapter by suggesting that there are perhaps two different concepts of self-evidence: one guarantees truth while the other does not. If this is so, we can see how it is not accurate to lump memory together with awareness of self-evident truths of logic as species of the same kind of intuitive knowledge.

▶ 12 Truth and falsehood

It is interesting to note that it is not until his twelfth chapter that Russell turns to the question of truth and falsehood. This reflects the fact that philosophy involves a lot of ground work before someone like Russell can finally address the question of what truth is.

In Russell's division between types of knowledge, truth and falsehood does not even arise as an issue when it comes to knowledge by acquaintance. As he says: 'We may draw wrong inferences from our acquaintance, but the acquaintance itself cannot be deceptive.' Statements and propositions, however, which are the stuff of knowledge by description, can be true or false and so this chapter focuses on this part of knowledge.

But there is even more narrowing of scope. Russell defers the question of how we know whether something is true or false to the next chapter. Here, he sticks to the question of what we *mean* when we say a proposition is true or false. This may seem like an unnecessary delay. But this focus on what we mean by key concepts is distinctive of a lot of philosophy in the English-speaking world over the last hundred years. Far from being an evasion, it is perhaps best seen as a recognition that we cannot say anything with confidence unless we first understand precisely what we mean by what we say.

Russell argues that any credible explanation of what truth and falsehood are must meet three conditions. First, it must account for the existence of both truth *and* falsehood. These are two sides of the same coin, so any theory of truth must also include an account of falsehood. Second, it must involve belief. Without beliefs there is nothing to be true or false. Third, the truth or falsehood of a belief must depend on something outside the belief itself. If, for example, I say that Paris is the capital of France, the truth of this statement is determined by facts outside the belief, not by the nature of the belief itself.

This third condition implies what is known as the correspondence theory of truth. That is to say, a proposition is true if it corresponds accurately to the way things actually are, and is false if it fails to so correspond. Although this may sound like common sense, it is actually very difficult to unpack what is meant by 'correspondence'. For this reason, alternative theories of truth have been offered.

Russell considers only one here: the coherence theory. According to this, propositions are true or false in so far as they cohere with other views which are themselves accepted as true and false. On this view, truth is determined holistically: the truth of any individual proposition cannot be assessed independently of considering its place in a wider system of propositions.

Russell is unimpressed by this theory for two reasons. First of all, he thinks it is possible that two or more different, conflicting bodies of belief may both cohere. In one such body, for example, the sun may be thought to orbit the Earth, and in another, the Earth be thought to orbit the sun. On the coherence theory, we would have no reason to prefer one body of beliefs over the other. Russell thinks this is crazy, because if two statements directly contradict each other only one can be true.

This links with his second objection. The idea of coherence presupposes basic truths of logic. These truths of logic are not accepted because they cohere with other truths, but because they are self-evidently true. So the coherence theory itself rests on deeper foundations than mere coherence. In other words, it implicitly acknowledges that there is more to truth, at root, than mere coherence.

We might add that the coherence theory presupposes the laws of logic, and yet it allows that two directly contradictory propositions may be true, so long as they both belong to coherent bodies of belief. In this way, the theory can be seen to be self-defeating: it rests on basic logical principles such as the law of contradiction, but according to the law on contradiction two conflicting bodies of belief accepted as true by the theory cannot both be true after all.

For these reasons, Russell rejects the coherence theory and returns to correspondence. Coherence, he argues, is a mark of truth, but not the defining characteristic of it.

So how does Russell manage to make sense of the idea of correspondence? He does so in an ingenious and original way. The key to his account harks back to what he said in Chapter 10 (see the section above on our knowledge of universals) about philosophy paying too much attention to things and too little attention to the relations between them. In this case, the upshot of that is that Russell sees true belief as being a correspondence of relations.

Russell uses a literary example to make his point. What would make Othello's belief that 'Desdemona loves Cassius' true? What does Othello's belief need to correspond to in order for it to be true? The short answer is that the belief is true if there is what Russell calls a 'complex' which corresponds to this belief. The complex in this case would involve three things: Desdemona, Cassius and loving. Further, this complex is arranged in a certain way, so that the loving is directed from Desdemona to Cassius. In this way, correspondence of belief is not just a correspondence of words to their objects, but also a correspondence of the relations between the words and the relations between the objects they refer to.

Put more technically, Russell calls Desdemona and Cassius the object-terms and the loving the object-relation. A belief is true if the object-terms and object-relations exist in the same order as in the belief; it is false if they do not.

Although this is more sophisticated than many versions of the correspondence theory, it still suffers from the same fundamental weakness. That is to say, how do we explain how words correspond to things? By what process do these words connect with objects in the real world? There is something mysterious in this which Russell's theory, for all its elegance and ingenuity, fails to remove.

▶ 13   Knowledge, error and probable opinion

Having dealt with what makes beliefs true or false, Russell now turns to the question of how we know what is true and false. His discussion centres on an account of knowledge that has its roots in Plato: the idea that knowledge is a form of justified true belief.

Holding a true belief by itself is not enough for knowledge. For example, I may come to believe that Italy will win the soccer World Cup just because I am a passionate supporter and always believe they will win. If they do win, my belief was true. But it would be crazy to say I knew they would win, since the method I used to acquire my belief is extremely unreliable and may lead me to acquire false beliefs on other occasions.

One way in which I might have a justified true belief is if my belief is validly deduced from true premises. But this won't do either, since I can reach true conclusion from true premises even when I do not know the premises to be true. For example, I may believe that Bonn is the capital of Germany and go on to deduce true beliefs from the true premise that the capital of Germany begins with the letter 'B'. One such true belief might be: 'The capitals of France and Germany do not begin with the same letter.' Here, I have deduced a true belief from true premises, but since at the root of this is the false belief that Bonn is the capital of Germany, how can I really be said to know the conclusion is true? It seems more accurate to say I was just lucky to end up with a true belief.

A further problem is that there are many things we surely do know, even though we did not come to believe them by a process of valid deduction. The human mind does not operate according to the rules of logic textbooks and it seems unnecessarily restrictive to insist that we only have knowledge when we reason in a particular way.

More fundamentally, such an account of knowledge can only deal with derivative knowledge: that which we come to acquire through a process of reasoning. But at the root of any derivative knowledge is intuitive knowledge, which we do not deduce. As we saw in Chapter 11 on intuitive knowledge, knowledge has to have foundations and those foundations are not derived from other truths but are intuitively known.

Taking all this into account, Russell offers a preliminary definition of derivative knowledge as true belief which is arrived at by any psychological inference which has a corresponding logical inference which could be spelled out. The reader may well wish to consider whether this is an adequate account for themselves, but as it is only a preliminary definition, we will not consider its adequacy here.

Russell, however, is keener to deal with the problem of intuitive knowledge, as this is more basic than the derivative variety. Remember, in the last chapter Russell argued that beliefs were true when they had a corresponding complex. These complexes, argues Russell, can be known in two ways. Consider the example of 'Desdemona loves Cassius'. This is a complex which Desdemona, and Desdemona alone, can know by acquaintance. For everyone else, knowledge can only be gained by making a judgement that the complex does, in fact, obtain. Judgement, however, is always fallible. So the truth of 'Desdemona loves Cassius', or any complex, is only self-evident to those in a position to be directly acquainted with it.

Facts about universals have the advantage that anyone can be directly acquainted with them. Anyone can be acquainted with the complex '$1 + 1 = 2$' whereas only Desdemona can be acquainted with the complex 'Desdemona loves Cassius'.

Russell maintains that although the self-evidence which comes from direct acquaintance with a fact or complex is 'an absolute guarantee of truth', and he also maintains that in any particular instance we cannot be absolutely certain that our judgement is true. In this, Russell returns again to the idea that self-evidence is a matter of degree, as is, by implication, the idea of knowledge.

In the penultimate paragraph of this chapter Russell provides a useful taxonomy of knowledge, with the most certain type of knowledge first:

We can be most certain that we have knowledge in the cases of sense data and simple truths of logic and arithmetic. More complex logic or mathematics is known with less certainty. Truths derived from what is intuitively known are also less and less certain the greater the number of deductive steps from that which is intuitively known they are.

What does this mean for knowledge? Well, at one end of the spectrum, that which we come to believe by intuition (in Russell's sense) or that which we come to believe from such intuitive truths by a reliable method of inference, we call knowledge. That which we believe but is not true, we call error. That which we believe is true, but is neither intuitively known nor derived from highly reliable methods of inference, we call probable opinion.

This is a thorough and impressive account of knowledge, but it does leave many loose ends. In particular, there is a question mark over what constitutes a reliable method of inference. Russell has already stated that it is too narrow to confine derivative knowledge to that which we arrive at by deduction. But what other mechanisms of thought are acceptable? This question is left unanswered, which means Russell's account of knowledge is left incomplete here.

▶ 14   The limits of philosophical knowledge

Anyone reading *The Problems of Philosophy* hoping to find proofs for religious beliefs, the illusoriness of matter or the unreality of evil will be sorely disappointed. Russell claims that big metaphysical questions such as these cannot be answered by philosophy. In this chapter Russell does two things. First, he discusses Hegel as an example of an attempt to answer such questions which fails. Second, he then goes on to explain in general why it is that philosophy can never answer such questions.

Hegel's fundamental theory was that everything except the whole is fragmentary and cannot exist independently. Hegel compares the philosopher to the anatomist. Just as the anatomist examines a single bone to see what the whole animal is like, so a philosopher examines one piece of reality to see what reality as a whole is like. In both cases, the part can only be understood fully when considered in the context of the whole it comes from. Hegel's theory thus asserts the fundamental interconnectedness of all things, and of all thoughts.

Hegel devised a method of reasoning which he called the dialectic method. This has three stages.

The starting point is an idea, or *thesis*. If any idea is considered on its own, it will be found to be incomplete. If we press the idea hard enough, we will end up with a contradiction, the opposite of the original idea which is its *antithesis*. This contrary idea will also turn out to be incomplete and will end up in contradiction. However, by combining what is true of the thesis and antithesis and ditching what is untrue, we arrive at the *synthesis*. This is a new idea that is less incomplete than the preceding thesis and antithesis. However, it will usually be the case that this synthesis will become the thesis for a new dialectical movement which repeats the process once more. The process of thesis–antithesis–synthesis thus continues until we reach the Absolute idea, which is complete and without contradiction. This is the true, harmonious reality.

Great though this sounds, Russell believes it to be wrong. The main reason for this comes in Hegel's idea of what makes something incomplete. Hegel claims that whatever has relations to things outside itself must contain some reference to those outside things in its own nature, and couldn't be what it is if those outside things didn't exist. For example, a man's nature involves what he knows, loves, desires and so on. So he couldn't be what he is without those things he knows, loves, desires and so on. Therefore, he is a fragment, a part of a whole which includes all those external things upon which his own nature depends.

On this view, the 'nature' of a thing is 'everything true of that thing'. This clearly does include all the things it is related to in the universe, which is just everything. For example, as I am 300 miles from Paris, I have a relation with Paris, namely the relation of being 300 miles from it.

But this view seems crazy. Surely 'nature' means something like the essential qualities of a thing. It seems that there are many relations a thing has which are not necessary for it to be the thing it is. I would be the same if I were not 300 miles from Paris, for example. Also, I can know something well by acquaintance and not know all its relations. Does this mean I do not know its nature? Surely I know the nature of my pain as well as anyone, even though I am ignorant of its many relations.

In summary, Russell denies Hegel's claim that in order to know something fully, one must know all its relations. Many relations, it seems, are not part of the nature of a thing at all. Once this is denied, the foundation of Hegel's system disappears.

Hegel's failure is symptomatic of the general failure of grand metaphysical systems of philosophy. Metaphysicians have often tried to show that apparent features of the world are self-contradictory and therefore not real. For example, the Achilles and the Tortoise paradox is supposed to show that, although space and time appear infinitely divisible, they cannot be so. However, modern mathematics has shown, in turn, that the philosophical arguments used in these cases are also fallacious.

Also, philosophers have tried to show the *a priori* necessity of the nature of space and time. But now, we have proofs that other spaces are equally possible, and that observation cannot confirm which space we actually occupy.

What these examples show is that it is very difficult, if not impossible, to prove the nature of reality by philosophical argument. The more we know, the more our knowledge of what is appears to have shrunk, whilst our knowledge of what might be has increased. Logic, therefore, rather than limiting what is possible until we are left with only one possible world, actually leaves many options open to us. A great deal is logically possible. We have to use experience to decide which of these logical possibilities our world actually conforms to.

We do this by a combination of experience and *a priori* principles. For example, the law of gravitation requires experience of seeing things always falling and it requires the inductive principle, which is *a priori* (as it cannot be confirmed or denied by experience).

Russell claims that we have two types of intuitive knowledge. The first is pure *a priori* knowledge, the second is pure empirical knowledge. Knowledge we derive from these intuitions always requires some pure *a priori* knowledge and usually requires some pure empirical knowledge as well.

Because all knowledge is derived in this way, philosophy is not essentially different from any other forms of knowledge, such as science. The key difference is that philosophy is critical, putting ideas and principles under the microscope and examining them for contradictions and coherence. In this, Russell may be a little off the mark. Other disciplines are also critical. Perhaps what distinguishes philosophy is rather the kinds of questions it asks, questions which do not have determinate answers.

We cannot, however, be pure sceptics. We cannot step outside the circle of knowledge, as all refutations must begin with some piece of knowledge which disputants share. Cartesian scepticism is, for example, a constructive scepticism. If philosophy sticks to this role, it will help reduce error and it is in this that some of the value of philosophy lies.

▶ 15 The value of philosophy

Why study philosophy? In the final chapter of *The Problems of Philosophy*, Russell addresses this very question.

Philosophy is often accused of being useless because it has no practical effects. Science, engineering and medicine all help improve the quality of our lives, but what does philosophy do? This criticism is misplaced because though what is practical satisfies our material needs, those are not the only needs we have. We also have mental needs, needs to understand ourselves and the world, and our place in it.

Another difference between philosophy and 'practical' subjects is that the benefits of philosophy are primarily for the student of philosophy and do not filter through to society as a whole. Whereas a cure for cancer benefits many, one's own philosophical development doesn't much affect others. There are certain exceptions to this which Russell doesn't consider. Utilitarianism, for example, greatly influenced political thinking in the late nineteenth century and thus did affect the lives of many.

One reason why philosophy is often called upon to defend its value is its apparent lack of success. If you ask a philosopher what definite body of truths has been ascertained by philosophy, if she is honest, the answer will be quite short. There are two reason for this. First, where success in philosophy has occurred, it has tended to lead to the creation of new, separate subjects. Virtually all the subjects we study were at one time classed as philosophy. This justifies the historical value of philosophy, but doesn't say too much about philosophy today. Second, those questions that remain within philosophy tend not to admit of definite answers. It is not only true, for example, that we have not yet discovered what the true basis of ethics is, it is almost certain that we could never say with any certainty what it is. Philosophy helps us to clarify these questions, understand their importance and so on as much as it does provide answers.

Given this, it would be unwise to see the value of philosophy as depending upon any supposed body of definitely ascertainable knowledge. On the contrary, Russell believes the uncertainty philosophy promotes is the very key to its value. Once we realise the multitude of possibilities and lack of certainties, we are freed from an unquestioning, prejudiced life and our thoughts are 'freed from the tyranny of custom'. As we come to see that there is more in heaven and earth than we may have believed, we enlarge our interests and concerns. Russell goes so far as to say that the unphilosophic life is 'feverish and confined', whereas the philosophic life is 'calm and free'.

Russell explains this in terms of self and not-self. When we see everything from the point of view of ourselves, we not only fail to see all that there is, but we actually confine the self to those things of which it is directly aware. When we begin to see the world more impersonally, we also actually enlarge the self, because we make much more available to our understanding and comprehension. It sounds paradoxical, but Russell is saying that the way to truly enlarge the self is to first of all deny the self its central role.

Therefore, views which say that man is the measure of all things are not only wrong, but, if true, they would rob philosophy of its real value – the ability to take us beyond our own experience. Philosophy, then, aspires to an almost God-like view from nowhere, where the world is understood not from any particular viewpoint, but from a neutral perspective.

By enlarging the objects of our understanding, we also enlarge the objects of our actions and affections. It makes us 'citizens of the universe' in which 'consists man's true freedom'.

Russell, in contrast to the cool, detached tone of the book so far, thus ends with an almost mystical passage in which the self is enlarged and achieves a kind of union with the universe. In a way, this is not surprising. Many people who study abstract disciplines like maths or theoretical physics feel the same way. It is precisely because philosophy is at times abstract that we can go beyond our particular, concrete concerns.

Summary

Our knowledge of the world is not based on our awareness of objects themselves, since all we directly perceive are **sense data**. Although we believe that these sense data correspond to independently existing matter, we have no proof for this. It is merely the best explanation for why we perceive sense data as we do. We have good reasons to think that this matter is ordered in time and space more or less as we perceive it, but we cannot access the full reality behind appearances. Since all we are aware of are mental entities, **idealists** have suggested that only mental entities exist. This, argues Russell, is because they fail to realise that while *awareness* must be mental, what we are *aware of* need not be.

We know things in one of two ways: by **acquaintance** and **description**. Descriptions can be definite (the so and so) or indefinite (a so and so). Proper names, like Paris or Winston Churchill, are shorthand for definite descriptions.

The things we can know by acquaintance are sense data, memories, the contents of our minds through introspection, **universals** and possibly ourselves. Universals are the general concepts which all particular things fall under. For example, 'bear' is the universal of which Winnie the Pooh is a particular example. Universals are real but not material.

All *a priori* knowledge deals exclusively with the relations of universals. This is why *a priori* knowledge can never tell us anything about the nature of the real world. This, in turn, is why past philosophical attempts to construct *a priori* accounts of the whole of reality have failed. General principles, such as the laws of logic, are derived from experience, but their proof does not depend on facts about the world, so they are *a priori*.

Knowledge of the world is based on **induction**. This is reasoning based on the principle that if two things are found to be associated with each other and never found disassociated from each other, then the more cases we have of them associated, the greater is the probability that they will continue to be associated in the future. The principle cannot be established by rational argument but it is indispensable.

All reasoning rests on basic intuitions which cannot themselves be proved by reason. These intuitions are **self-evident truths**, but there are degrees of self-evidence, so not all such truths are beyond doubt.

Russell supports the **correspondence theory** of truth and argues that a belief is true if the terms and relations exist in the world in the same order as in the belief.

Knowledge, therefore, is that which we come to believe by intuition or that which we come to believe from such intuitive truths by a reliable method of inference. That which we believe, is true, but is not intuitively known nor derived from highly reliable methods of inference, we call probable opinion.

Glossary

A priori From first principles, the truth of which are established independently of experience.

Correspondence theory A theory which states that a sentence or utterance is true if and only if it corresponds to reality.

Idealism The theory that everything that exists is mental in nature.

Induction Reasoning from particular facts obtained from experience to other particular facts or general laws.

Knowledge by acquaintance Knowledge gained by direct experience of the thing known (e.g. by sense experience).

Knowledge by description Knowledge of things not directly experienced, which is built up from things known by acquaintance.

Self-evident truths Truths which do not need to be justified by appeal to other truths or arguments, such as basic rules of logic and mathematics.

Sense data What we are immediately aware of in experience through the senses, such as colours, shapes, smells and textures.

Universals General concepts which do not describe particular objects, but a quality shared by several particular objects (e.g. whiteness).

Further reading

The Problems of Philosophy is published by Oxford University Press.

Russell and Whitehead's *Principia Mathematica* (Cambridge University Press) is inaccessible to all but the specialist and is best avoided. *The Basic Writings of Bertrand Russell* or *Bertrand Russell's Best* (Routledge) are better first steps if you want to read more of his own work.

Russell's *History of Western Philosophy* (Routledge) is as much about Russell as anyone else and is still considered a classic.

Ray Monk's two volumes of biography, *Bertrand Russell: The Spirit of Solitude* and *Bertrand Russell: The Ghost of Madness* (Vintage) are both gripping reads and present Russell warts and all, to the chagrin of many of Russell's admirers. Monk also contributed the volume on *Russell* to the *Great Philosophers* series (Phoenix) and it is also part of the anthology, *The Great Philosophers*, edited by Monk and Fredric Raphael (Phoenix).

5 Jean-Paul Sartre: *Existentialism and Humanism* (1947)

▶ Background

Jean-Paul Sartre is one of the most famous philosophers of the twentieth century. In addition to being a major writer of philosophy, he was also a novelist, playwright and an important social and political commentator, both in his native France and internationally.

His reputation today, however, is mixed. He has fallen somewhat out of fashion in France, where once he was an idol. In Britain and America, his public fame is not always matched by his reputation among academics. In part this is because of the cultural divide between so-called Anglo-American 'analytic' philosophy and 'Continental' philosophy. How deep the differences between the two traditions run is a matter of dispute. But its effect has been to keep Sartre off the syllabuses of many university philosophy courses.

Sartre is usually described as an existentialist philosopher. What it means to be an existentialist is one of the questions Sartre raises in *Existentialism and Humanism*. One of the most striking features of existentialism is the wide variety of opinions held by its figureheads. Søren Kierkegaard is usually considered to be the father of existentialism, and he was a devout Christian. Martin Heidegger was an existentialist who supported the Nazi regime in Germany. Sartre, on the other hand, was a left-wing atheist. This wide disagreement may seem odd, but it is perhaps an inevitable consequence of existentialism's defining feature.

All existentialists stress human freedom to choose. We find ourselves in the world confronted by big questions. Why are we here? Is there a creator? What should my life's objective be? What are my moral values? Throughout history, people have argued that these questions can be settled for good. Through recourse either to religious faith, authority, or the power of reason, these are questions which have answers which, once understood, are there just for us to accept.

What the existentialists stress is that nothing can settle these questions other than human free will. Whatever the evidence, it is always inconclusive and we are left having to decide for ourselves. For example, Kierkegaard tells of the story of Abraham, who was asked by God to sacrifice his only son. God's will could be

115

seen as providing an objective moral law. On this view, Abraham wouldn't need to choose what is right, he would just have to obey God. But Kierkegaard argued Abraham *did* have to make his own choices. How did Abraham know this was God speaking to him? How did he decide he ought to obey God, even though he was being commanded to do something which by all moral standards was wrong? The evidence couldn't settle these questions one way or another. Abraham had to choose for himself. This placed a lot of power and responsibility on his own free will. Abraham's case is extreme, but Kierkegaard's point is that we too have to rely on our own free will – what we must do is not set out clearly for us.

The problem is particularly acute when it comes to moral values. You can't prove that, for example, murder is wrong, in the same way you can prove $1 + 1 = 2$, or that water is H_2O. Values have to be chosen. This is again a great responsibility for human freedom.

So what unites existentialists is their view that we have to choose and that our choices cannot be seen as inevitable, or determined by the facts. That is why different existentialists could have chosen different values and still all been existentialists.

▶ **The text**

Existentialism and Humanism must be read carefully for several reasons. First, it is in fact a public speech Sartre gave rather than a detailed philosophical work. It is designed to put over some key points in an accessible way to a wide audience. For that reason, it is perhaps unfair to scrutinise it as if it were a complete argument.

Nevertheless, when reading any philosophical text, one has to examine the arguments as they are set out. *Existentialism and Humanism* is no exception. But we should be careful not to generalise from this one work to making judgements about Sartre's philosophy as a whole. Indeed, Sartre himself was said to have disowned the work later in life, dissatisfied with what it said.

A second reason for caution is that the book is in part an outline of a project Sartre never completed. Critics of existentialism complained that it had no place for moral values, or ethics. Sartre wanted to construct a coherent existentialist ethic and *Existentialism and Humanism* is in part a sketch of how he thought that ethic might look. But the project was never completed, which again gives us reason not to judge the book as a completed work of philosophy.

The book remains of great interest, however, because it is Sartre's clearest and most accessible writing on his own philosophy. His magnum opus, *Being and Nothingness*, is a huge and difficult work. *Existentialism and Humanism* is, in contrast, short and easy to read, but still direct from the pen of one of philosophy's finest.

▶ The attack on existentialism

Existentialism and Humanism begins with an outline of its purpose. It is clear that one of the main aims of the book is to defend existentialism against its critics. The first criticism he cites is that existentialism leads to quietism, the belief that one should do nothing because nothing one can do can change anything. On this view, existentialism is a philosophy of despair which can provide no hope for life. As Sartre's comments make clear, this criticism was particularly made by the communists. They believed that human action was necessary to end the subjugation of the working classes by the bourgeoisie. Inaction, which they thought followed from existentialism, is therefore reactionary, a means only of sustaining the current, unjust *status quo.*

The second accusation is that existentialism debases humanity. This is because existentialism emphasises the individual. Your choice and your free will are of central importance. You can only see the world from your point of view and you cannot rely on other people to give your life value or meaning. This, it was claimed, led to solipsism – the view that each person is essentially alone, and that the world only exists from their viewpoint. In Descartes's famous phrase, a person is essentially a 'cogito' – an 'I think' – and is thus in essence a private mind, separated from others by her subjectivity.

A third accusation is that existentialism leads to a lack of values, where everything is permitted and no-one can be condemned. After all, if values have to be chosen by each individual, how can they really be moral values at all? Isn't it the point of moral values that they apply to everyone, not that they are things we just choose for ourselves?

Whether or not you judge *Existentialism and Humanism* to be a successful work of philosophy depends to a large part on whether you think it successfully answers these criticisms.

▶ Humanism

Sartre now moves on to discuss the second word in his lecture's title: humanism. Traditionally, humanism is the view that 'man is the measure of all things', and that humanity is in control of its own destiny. Humanists claim that all humans are part of one brotherhood and that without God's help, we can achieve progress.

It is perhaps because humanism is optimistic and existentialism is perceived as pessimistic that the combination of the two seems surprising. But it is clear there is a large overlap between them. Both put people at the centre of their own destinies and both can do without God (although, as we have seen, there are religious existentialists). However, where Sartre believes they part is that existentialism leaves the individual with responsibility for her own actions and destiny, denying that she can rely on other people to help her, whereas the humanist believes in human solidarity almost as a given. What the humanist takes on faith – progress and the family of man – the existentialist warns cannot be taken for granted.

Sartre tries to overturn the preconception that existentialism is pessimistic and humanism optimistic. People believe existentialism is pessimistic (and hence anti-humanist) because it denies a universal human nature and it is our common human nature that provides hope for shared values and enterprises. But, in fact, how often is human nature attributed as the cause of all kinds of wrongdoing? Conservative belief is that human nature is base and self-seeking and that only the constraints of a civilised society can keep it in check. How, Sartre asks, can existentialism, which denies this inherent evil and claims we have the freedom to choose our own destinies, be considered pessimistic compared to this?

The unstated conclusion of this part of the book is that existentialism is humanist because it puts humanity at centre stage, master of itself, even though each human is taken as an autonomous individual, as compared to the homogeneous 'humanity' of traditional humanism.

▶ Existentialism

Having considered humanism, in a key section Sartre then defines and explains what existentialism is. As Sartre defines existentialism, the central point is that, for human beings, '*existence* comes before *essence*, or if you will, that we must begin with the subjective'. Sartre chooses, perhaps misleadingly, to discuss essence in terms of an artefact and its creator. An artefact, such as a paper-knife, is created with specific functions in mind. What is more, the knife itself obviously cannot alter that function. The essence of the knife is thus its purpose and function, what is was made for. This essence came before its existence, as it was created *for* a particular purpose. If God existed, humans too would be like this. God would have created humanity with a specific essence. We would possess a human nature which God himself had put there. This nature would comprise our essence, and so our essence would precede our existence.

But Sartre denies that God exists. If God does not exist, humanity has no creator, and if it has no creator it has no predetermined essence. Rather, humanity first exists, and then as its self awareness increases, the individual confronts herself, and is able to choose, to will for herself her own nature, purposes and values. In this way, humanity's existence precedes essence. 'There is no human nature, because there is no God to have a conception of it.'

We should be careful not to assume that what Sartre says of his own existentialism is true of all existentialists. If we take Sartre's definition as applying to all existentialism, it comes up against some serious objections. First, one can be an existentialist and believe in God. As we have seen, it was Kierkegaard who really founded existentialism, and he believed in God. So what made him an existentialist? He believed that reason could never provide answers to ultimate questions of meaning and purpose in human life, which meant that we have to choose for ourselves, in an act of faith, what to believe in. Hence, it is the impotence of reason and the importance of subjective choice which are crucial to his being an existentialist. So whereas Sartre starts from God's non-existence and ends up with man's abandonment, Kierkegaard *begins* with man's abandonment, seeing this as part of the human condition whether God exists or not. This shows how the non-existence of God is not vital to the key existentialist belief that we must choose for ourselves.

A second objection is more specifically directed at how Sartre constructs his argument about essence. It seems clear that something can have an essence which it can't choose, even if there is no God. If God does not exist, that means nobody created trees and prawns, for example. Does that mean their existence precedes their essences? That would be absurd. Essence seems to be connected with purpose or a creator only in the case of artefacts. In natural objects, such as animals and plants, essence is just the essential properties of a thing. What makes humanity different is our ability to choose for ourselves. It is for this reason that man's existence precedes his essence, not because there is no God.

Sartre makes much of the idea that there is no human nature. As we have seen, even without God, things can have a nature, so why not humans? Certainly, we have something like freedom of choice, but there may be certain features of humans as a species like any other which are just there, whether we like them or not. Anthropologists would probably support the view that there are some characteristics which all humans share, which could fairly be called human nature. Bear this in mind in later arguments where the non-existence of human nature is assumed.

▶ Subjectivity

The unimportance of God is perhaps supported by Sartre's claims about the importance of subjectivity in existentialism. Our subjectivity is the way in which we perceive the world from a particular point of view. My thoughts, feelings and perceptions are all located 'in' me, which gives me a set of private 'inner' states – the subjective – which is separate from the public, 'outer' world of objects.

It is the fact that humans possess a subjective life which marks them out from other things and places on them responsibility for what they are. A tin can cannot be responsible because it has no view of the world. It just *is*. We, however, can think and feel and this enables us to decide what we want to do and who we want to be. This places responsibility on us for those choices and freedoms.

But our responsibility extends beyond our own being. Sartre argues that when we choose for ourselves, we also choose for all others. The reasons for this are deceptively simple: when we choose how we want to be, we are fashioning an image of mankind as we believe it ought to be. To choose one way is to affirm the value of what is chosen.

The idea is simply that by doing something we are condoning it, and we cannot consistently condone it for ourselves but not for all others as well. For example, if I don't pay my bus fare, I am effectively saying it's okay for anyone in a similar situation not to pay bus fares. My choice for me contains within it an implied recommendation or endorsement of the action for others. Hence, to choose for all humanity is not to impose one's will upon it, but merely to choose how one would want other people to be.

Although what Sartre says seems to make sense, it perhaps contradicts one of his basic tenets, namely that there is no universal human nature. If all people are alike, then when I choose for myself it follows that, to be consistent, I am choosing what I think would be best for anyone. But if there is no human nature, then all people are not alike and free to choose whatever they want. In that case, I can consistently argue that what I choose for myself is irrelevant for others, as I see that each person makes their own essence. If someone chooses as I do, I should be neither approving nor reproachful, because he is different to me in different circumstances, so it is impossible for me to say whether he chose wisely or not. Hence, it does seem possible to fashion oneself whilst in no way condoning anything for other people.

A further criticism is that even if we accept that by choosing for myself I assert that my action is permissible, it by no means follows that I am actively seeking to fashion how others should be. It is like the difference between enjoying music and claiming that everyone should enjoy music. Thus, even if Sartre is right, our responsibility is perhaps not so great as he would have us believe. So long as we do nothing which we think should never be done, what we choose only adds to the list of permissible actions, not to what should be done. There is a gap between 'may' and 'ought'. Just because I think something *may* be done, it doesn't mean I think it *ought* to be done.

▶ Anguish

What follows from our responsibility for our actions is anguish. Anguish is what a person feels when she is confronted with a choice, fully realising that when she chooses, she chooses for all, like a legislator for humankind. Anguish is thus the sense of 'profound responsibility' felt. Sartre asserts that everyone either feels anguish, disguises it or is in flight from it, but that no-one can escape it altogether.

Sartre echoes Kierkegaard by illustrating anguish with the story of Abraham, who is told by an angel to sacrifice his own son. The problem Abraham faces is that only he can decide whether it really is an angel, whether he really is delivering God's will and so on. Could it not be a malicious demon? Think of all the serial killers propelled by commanding voices. However Abraham decides, he will be asserting his choice for others (particularly his son!). How does he deal with such responsibility? Sartre also gives the example of military leaders, whose decisions will affect the fates of thousands.

This anguish is not a call to quietism, to do nothing. It is rather a condition of action. It is only because we do have choices that we can act at all. Without choices, our actions are merely mechanical. But with choice comes anguish. Of course, if we don't really choose for all humanity, then Sartre's anguish is avoidable in all but the cases where our actions have a direct result on others (see previous section). It is no coincidence that Sartre's examples of Abraham and generals are of this sort, because in such cases the anguish seems so hard to avoid. We would be less convinced by an example of a person deciding whether or not to obey a 'do not walk on the grass' sign.

Sartre's claim that we all feel, flee or deny our anguish is a very dubious one for two main reasons. How do we assess Sartre's claim that everyone falls into one of these three categories? Certainly, Sartre's idea would explain why so many people don't show this anguish, but then, unless he has good reasons for backing up his claim, his thesis is empty.

We can see what is dubious in his claim by considering an exact analogy. What if I were to claim that everyone loves toffee, disguises their love for toffee or is in flight from their love for it? Of course, if anyone denied they loved toffee, my theory would explain that denial. But unless I have good reasons to suppose my theory is true, it is empty. No evidence would either support or refute it. Furthermore, because anguish is an emotional reaction, the only way to show all people felt it would surely be through empirical psychology. It is clear, however, that the only psychology in Sartre is of the armchair variety. Throughout *Existentialism and Humanism*, there are a number of claims which are of this armchair psychology variety. This means assessing them is very difficult. If, from our armchairs, people's minds appear as they do to Sartre, we are likely to agree with him; if not, then we won't. But this kind of judgement is philosophically unsatisfactory. Since Sartre claims there is no human nature, generalising from our limited experience to that of all people seems particularly unreasonable.

This leads into the second reason why Sartre's account of anguish is dubious: it claims a kind of reaction is universal to everyone when there is no universal human nature. Perhaps we need to read Sartre more carefully. Sartre claims here that human nature cannot be ascribed *a priori*. If something follows *a priori*, it means that you do not need to appeal to experience to demonstrate its truth. In this context, it means that human nature is not a given, handed down from above or something which exists by necessity. Could human nature therefore be ascribed *a posteriori*? In other words, is it possible to ascribe certain universal human characteristics based on experience and observation of human behaviour?

There are two problems for this. The first is that this would severely water down what Sartre seems usually to be saying, namely that there is no human nature, full stop – *a priori* or *a posteriori*. Second, Sartre provides no evidence from experience for his claim that everyone fits into the three categories of feeling, fleeing or denying their anguish. The claim thus seems baseless – he simply offers it up to us to accept or reject, based on our own experience. This is, perhaps, fully within the spirit of existentialism, which denies the power of reason to provide objective answers to the important questions in life, but it also demonstrates how hard it is to assess existentialism's claims.

▶ Abandonment

Sartre sees 'abandonment as no more than drawing out the logical consequences of God's non-existence'. This is where Sartre's existentialism differs from traditional humanism. The humanists claimed that, though God did not exist, or is not worth believing in, there could still be *a priori* moral values which society could follow. Removing God would thus leave our moral framework more or less intact. Sartre, on the contrary, believes that without God there cannot be any *a priori* values. For where would these values come from? There is no human nature to derive them from, as our existence precedes our essence. Nor is there any world other than our own, where objective moral rules are set out in metaphorical tablets of stone. Without moral rules either inscribed in human nature or in the natural fabric of the universe, we are truly abandoned, 'condemned to be free'. The odd conjunction of the ideas of condemnation and freedom is a product of the fact that we are born without any say in the matter (hence condemned), but thereafter free to choose our own destiny.

There is one other way in which we could deny our freedom, namely through determinism. Determinism is the thesis that human free will is an illusion. When we decide, for example, to choose a cup of tea instead of a coffee, we feel that our choice is a free one. That is to say, we feel sure that we could have chosen otherwise. However, the determinist argues that this feeling deceives us. In fact, the choice we made is somehow inevitable. How is this so?

In nature, we are familiar with the idea that nothing happens without a cause. If a tree falls down, we suppose it is because there was a strong wind, or because its roots had decayed, or something else which would explain it. The wind or the decayed roots would itself have a cause and so on. In short, we suppose that every event is the consequence of a complex chain of prior causes.

Are humans any different? Some would argue that we too are part of nature. We are organic beings. What we see and do comprises physical events, such as talking or moving an arm. These physical events are caused by events in the brain. These events too must be caused by something else and so on. Such reasoning can lead us to conclude that human actions, just like events in the physical world, are the consequence of prior causes. It may seem to us that a decision to choose tea is a free action, but that choice is as much part of the causal chain of nature as a tree falling over.

If all our actions are determined, it is hard to see how we can truly choose or be responsible. But Sartre rejects determinism, using passion as an example. Many people claim that they could not help what they did, because they were swept away by passion of one sort or another. This is one way of saying that their actions were not freely chosen, but part of some causal chain over which they had no control. Sartre claims this is little more than an excuse. He follows a line of reasoning which echoes Aristotle (see Chapter 1 on his *Ethics*), who claimed that we are doubly responsible for actions committed when drunk: we are to blame for putting ourselves into a drunken state and for the subsequent action. The same could be said for passion. By the time we have been swept away by passion, we have effectively already made our choice. Our choices put us in a situation where passion would take effect, but as we chose to put ourselves in that position, we cannot avoid responsibility.

Sartre's psychology is compelling here. We all recognise the phenomenon of falling into temptation because we allow ourselves to be tempted. The problem Sartre has here is that he gives no argument against the deeper claims of determinism: he simply flatly denies it is true. Determinists would say that the fact that we feel free when making cool choices and don't feel free when swept away by a passion is beside the point. In neither case are we really free at all. Sartre seems to be simply saying that determinists are making excuses. This doesn't address their deeper philosophical concerns about the nature of causation and human action.

Of course, there is much that could be said about this issue. Consider Hume's compatibilism, for example, which claims that it can be true both that all our actions are the inevitable consequence of past causes and that we are in an important sense still free (see Chapter 3 on the *Enquiry*). There is also the belief that it is psychologically impossible to believe in determinism, and thus that we have to live as though it were not true. But as Sartre doesn't address these issues at all, we have to conduct the debate for ourselves – and it is a long debate.

Returning to abandonment, Sartre's example concerns a young man who goes to him for advice during the war: does he stay and look after his mother, to whom he is everything, or go to fight in the resistance, which has a nobler aim but a less certain outcome? Sartre's helpful advice is, 'you choose!' The point is that choosing is unavoidable. If we seek advice, we have to decide whether to act upon it. If we choose someone to choose for us, we have already chosen, for when we choose an advisor, we already have an idea of what that person will advise. If we choose an ethical system (religious, Kantian, utilitarian, etc.), we are responsible for that choice. And we also still have choices within that system. For example, if I choose a morality that says I must love my neighbour, do I best love my neighbour by looking after him or fighting for his country?

Sartre perhaps overstates the extent to which choices are always in the balance. Certainly, there are many choices which for the Christian, Kantian or utilitarian are very clear-cut. The point is surely more fundamental. We choose the system we follow, and therefore even if the system sets out clearly what we have to do, we have still made our choice.

A nagging concern about Sartre's account of freedom is whether or not he has really hit upon some deep truth or expressed a mere tautology. A tautology is a statement which appears to be informative, but in fact adds nothing to our understanding. For example, if we know what the word 'bachelor' means, the statement 'all bachelors are unmarried men' is a tautology. It appears to be telling us something about bachelors, but in fact it only says in other words what is already contained in the meaning of 'bachelor'. Is the fact that we have to choose ourselves a tautology? Anything I do, I do *myself*. The addition of the word 'myself' adds nothing to the meaning of 'I do'. This would be true even if God did exist. Abandonment is surely not just an expression of this tautology, but a statement of the extent to which we are alone. But are we as alone as Sartre says? If we count the advice of others, the help we get from ethical systems and so on, it becomes less clear that we are totally abandoned. Once we see the tautology involved in the statement 'man *himself* chooses', it becomes imperative to say what makes abandonment more than just this tautology.

Sartre also talks about the importance of action. It is only by doing something that I can really be said to believe in doing that thing. How do I know if I really want to do something? Only if I do it. If I don't do it, it shows it wasn't that important to me. For example, if I really want to write a novel, I will. If I don't, it shows that I didn't really want to do it at all. Thus, we only know our true feelings when we act. This means our actions reveal, to ourselves and others, our feelings. In this sense, actions come first, and thus we cannot consult our feelings to decide whether to act one way or another.

Sartre seems to be downplaying conflicts of feeling here. If the young man, for example, chooses to join the resistance, that doesn't show he doesn't want to help his mother, merely that he feels helping the resistance is more important. But as Sartre puts it, neither he, nor we, can ever know how much he felt for his mother if he chooses not to look after her. This seems to be a form of extreme behaviourism, the view that statements about our inner lives – our feelings, beliefs and so on – are no more than products of our outer actions. This seems implausible. Though it may be true that the way we act shows the hierarchy of our emotions – that is to say, which ones are stronger – that doesn't mean that the emotions we don't act on are not real and capable of being felt and consulted prior to action. Hence Sartre could be charged with overstating the importance of action over emotion.

▶ Despair

Despite his assertions that existentialism is an optimistic philosophy, Sartre claims that we should act without hope. Contrary to appearances, there is no contradiction here. We should act without hope in the sense that we cannot rely on others, or an inevitable tide of history, to achieve what we desire. 'Hope' here means hope that things will come to pass without our making them so. It is this which cannot be relied upon, for there is no determinism and no human nature, according to Sartre. One must limit oneself to what one can be sure of. But how can one strive for justice and so on if one has no faith in others, as what one can personally achieve is always limited? Sartre responds, 'one need not hope in order to undertake one's work.' Thus the despair of not being able to rely too much on others should not lead one to inaction.

On Sartre's view, one cannot blame circumstances for what one hasn't done. It is pointless to say, 'I could have done better in my exams if I had worked harder', as the fact is that one didn't work harder. Why attribute to someone the ability to do precisely what she hasn't done? To talk of the exams, for example, is to assume the person could have worked harder. But seeing as they didn't, what justifies this claim? Because 'you are nothing else but what you live', it is only by action that we make ourselves what we are. Hence, we have to act, despite the despair of not being able to count on others.

We can now understand what Sartre means by 'the sternness of our optimism.' We can be whatever we choose to be. We are not born heroes or cowards, which is a cause for optimism. But as each person is forced to choose their own destiny, this optimism is stern, as it forces each of us to act with despair, abandonment and anguish.

Once more, Sartre may be overstating the extent of our freedom. In what sense, for example, is the arachnophobe free to touch spiders? It is perhaps true that humans are freer than they believe themselves to be, but until they are made to realise this, they are truly constrained. For example, the psychiatrist can show to the arachnophobe that they are free to touch spiders, but until this is shown to them, they really are not free to do so. We often have to rely on others beyond our control to make us realise the true extent of our freedom, which means that we are not free to fully realise our own capacity for freedom.

▶ The *cogito*

The French philosopher René Descartes is most famous for his declaration '*cogito ergo sum*' – 'I think therefore I am'. Descartes casts a long shadow over all modern philosophy. The *cogito* argument is taken as establishing several things. One is that the essence of a person is to be a thinking thing (see Chapter 2 on the *Meditations*). That is to say, we are by nature creatures which have a private, inner mental life and a unique perspective on the world. There is something it feels like to be me, sitting here, whereas there is nothing it feels like for my pen to sit on the table.

The problem with this view is that it seems to erect a barrier between my private inner life and the outer world. As Sartre says: 'Outside of the Cartesian *cogito*, all objects are no more than probable.' As all you can be sure of, for example, is that you can see this book, you cannot be sure that the book actually exists outside your perceptions. It could be a figment of your imagination or perhaps you are dreaming. Even more worrying is that you cannot be sure other people have minds. When you talk to someone, all you are aware of are the words they say, the facial expressions they make and their bodily movements. How do you know that behind that, inside, they are genuinely thinking and feeling like you?

Sartre takes up some consequences of Descartes's *cogito* argument. Sartre believes it contains an elevating aspect: the *cogito* establishes that humanity uniquely is subject rather than mere object. This establishes us as separate from the material world. Where Sartre differs from Descartes, however, is that he claims: 'when we say "I Think" . . . we are just as certain of others as we are of ourselves.' We live in a world of 'intersubjectivity', where one's own subjective existence is dependent in some way on interacting with the subjective existence of others. Far from trapping us inside our own private subjectivity, the *cogito* opens us up to the subjectivity of others. As Sartre does not justify this radical amendment to Descartes, it is up to us to try and make sense of it.

One key idea is that of the 'intentionality' of mental states. This means that mental states are always *about* something, they always contain a reference to something other than themselves. Hence, to perceive a colour is to have the mental state – in this case an awareness – and what that awareness is *of*. There is always such an 'of-ness' to mental states. Thus, it could be argued that the very having of a mental state presupposes something other than the subject of the mental state: there is also what the awareness or perception is of. Perhaps Sartre is suggesting that a perception of another person is a perception of another mind. However, there is no reason why the thing the mental state is about or of may not itself be mental and private to the subject of thought. Hence, awareness of green, for example, may be awareness of a certain sense experience which is mental and private to the individual.

A further explanation may be that Sartre takes the existence of others to be a deep assumption, that is to say, though not *a priori* necessary, it is so integral a part of our thinking that it cannot be dispensed with. Compare this to Hume's view of cause and effect, being the idea that though cause and effect cannot be shown rationally to exist, it is so fundamental to our thinking that we cannot do without it (see Chapter 3 on his *Enquiry*). The existence of others could equally well be presupposed in virtually every thought we have.

Perhaps the most persuasive explanation comes from Sartre's writing in other work, where he talks about something he calls 'the look'. Imagine you are alone in a room. Suddenly, you realise that someone is looking at you through a keyhole. Your experience changes. You are suddenly aware of the look of another subject. This is not something you have to think about or justify through reason. You are aware of the other person as another being with a subjective perspective on the world. In this way, the existence of other minds is something that is justified, not through reason, but phenomenologically. That is to say, we experience other people *as* subjects of experience like ourselves. This makes some sense of Sartre saying: 'When we say "I Think" … we are just as certain of others as we are of ourselves.' This certainty comes from the way in which we experience others, not in our reasoning about them. Whether or not this provides genuine certainty or not is, of course, highly debatable.

▶ The human condition

The existence of others leads Sartre to talk about the human condition, as opposed to human nature. The human condition is the set of limitations placed upon humanity. This is very important, because it sounds as though Sartre is contradicting himself. There is no *a priori* human nature and humans are absolutely free, and yet the human condition places limits on humans which are partly *a priori*, in that all humans are born to work and die, and partly historical, in that we may be born slaves or kings, for example. But the contradiction, if it is there at all, is not so obvious. Human nature is determined by the individual, and as this is internal, is wholly within their control. The human condition is external, and thus not wholly within the individual's control. Any philosophy which doesn't acknowledge this would be doomed to absurdity. I cannot, for example, choose to be 9 feet tall, as my height is beyond my control.

Sartre talks about what is objective and subjective in the human condition. The human condition is objective because it applies to everyone. This is because we all have to live within limits of what is humanly possible and because we share many limits, we can understand others and the purposes they make for their lives. The human condition is also subjective, because, as individual beings with a subjective viewpoint on the world, we each have to live within these limits in our own ways and determine our own proposes.

His account of the human condition can thus be summarised as follows:

Objective	Subjective
Limits apply to all people	Limits have to be lived within by individual subjective beings
These objective limits enable us to understand others' purposes	Our purposes are determined wholly by ourselves

Is this a case of Sartre trying to have it both ways? Sartre's philosophy hinges upon subjectivism and individual choice, and yet he wants to defend existentialism against the charge of solipsism. The human condition is a way of grasping hold of an objective framework within which we can understand the subjective lives of other individuals. But there is a two-pronged dilemma here. If the human condition is only a matter of external limitations, how can this help us to understand others that well? After all, rats face many of the same external limitations as us, but we cannot relate to their purposes very well. If, on the other hand, the human condition is also about internal similarities (which Sartre says it is not), then hasn't the divide between the human condition and human nature been breached? The point is that this last possibility seems to accord most with our intuitive view. Surely the reason why we can understand the purposes of others from different times and places is not because they face the same external limitations (they often do not), but because we believe ourselves to be like them, which is to believe in a human nature.

▶ Does it matter what you do?

Sartre goes on to considers three more charges against existentialism, all of which are somehow based in its subjectivity. The first is that, as human choice is rooted in the subjective, with no absolute values, what one chooses is unimportant. Sartre's response is that as humans are fully responsible for their own actions, they cannot act solely out of caprice or fancy. All actions have consequences for which the agent is responsible, so there can be no *acte gratuit* or act without cost, as André Gide put it. For this reason, it matters very much how we choose. Add to this the idea that when one chooses one chooses for all humanity, and our choices matter even more.

Sartre compares moral choice to artistic creation. In both one is free to do what one wants, as there are no *a priori* values determining the outcome. However, this analogy rather plays into the hands of Sartre's critics. He says: 'we never speak of a work of art as irresponsible.' But if his analogy is good, then nor should we talk of moral choice as irresponsible, which seems to imply that it doesn't matter how we choose. Though it may matter to *me* if I paint well or badly, or how I choose, that is not very much of a reply to critics who say Sartre's view makes moral choices unimportant.

▶ Can you judge others?

If we are free to choose, then how can we ever judge others for how they choose? How can we condemn the Nazis or rapists, for example? Sartre's reply is that we cannot judge the substance of their decisions, but we can judge the basis on which they were made. Judgements should be made on the plane of free commitment, in good faith. To act in good faith is to act in full awareness of one's freedom to choose and awareness of how one's choice is also a choice for all humanity. If one does not choose on this basis, one is in self-deception, and one's choice will thus be founded on an error. Hence, one can make a logical, if not a value, judgement, on a person whose choices are made in bad faith, in other words, in denial of their freedom and responsibility. If someone chooses to deceive themselves, then that too can be criticised for being an act of self-deception.

But on top of this, there is also a moral judgement that can be made. To act in good faith is to assert the value of freedom not just for oneself, but also for all humanity. Therefore, all those who deny their freedom are denying the value of freedom and should be judged accordingly, as 'cowards' or 'scum'. This seems to be a claim which flies in the face of all Sartre has said. He notes, 'although the content of morality is variable, a certain form of this morality is universal'. This is the distinction between substantive ethics which concerns which actions are right or wrong (non-universal, according to Sartre) and non-substantive ethics (which Sartre says is universal) which concerns the nature of moral judgements, rather than their actual content. The universal form is acting freely, whereas the substantive content of our choices varies. But saying that he can judge others for denying their freedom is to claim that there is at least one substantive moral value that is universal and *a priori*, namely the value of acting freely. This is to make an exception to his own rule that no moral values are *a priori*, which he reasserts only the page before. Therefore, to be consistent, Sartre can only criticise the person of bad faith for their logical error, not their error of values.

All this fails to answer the key objection. The worry is that, for existentialists, all is permitted. Sartre has basically agreed with this, adding that we can criticise the way in which we choose. But unless he can show that choosing genocide, rape, torture and so on are logically incompatible with acting in good faith, the charge against existentialism will stick. And even if he can do this, surely we must insist that the torturer is not just making a logical error, but a moral one too. In this section, Sartre certainly does little to address these worries.

Sartre's example of Maggie Tulliver in *The Mill on the Floss* and Stendhal's character, La Sanservina, is supposed to show how two people in identical situations can make different choices and yet both be acting in good faith. He also shows how two people could make the same choices, but in bad faith. This is interesting, as it shows that actions alone do not determine values, which seems to contradict what Sartre says earlier (see the section on abandonment.) In this section, Sartre is basically saying that it is the spirit in which we undertake actions rather than the actions themselves which is important, whereas previously he said that 'the deeds that one does are of central importance, not the feelings that inform them.' It seems Sartre is treating values differently from reasons without a clear justification. Our private *reasons* are felt to be crucial for deciding whether we act in good faith or not, and yet private *emotions* can only be gauged through behaviour. This is not a formal contradiction, since there could be one rule for reasons and another for emotions. But without some justification for this distinction, it seems Sartre is inconsistent in what he counts as important.

▶ A case of give and take

Sartre addresses the criticism that the existentialist takes what they give. In other words, since we choose our own values, they cannot really be values. The whole point about moral values is that they are there, whether you choose to act on them or not. If you say values are chosen, you essentially stop them being values.

Sartre replies: 'I am very sorry that it should be so.' Without God, it cannot be any other way. Values have to be chosen because no God can choose them for us. In a sense, there is a stark choice. Either values are chosen by us or there are no values. Which you believe to be true will depend on whether you accept that values can be chosen and still be genuine values. There is little in this text to help us decide the matter.

▶ Humanism again

Sartre goes on to distinguish between good and bad humanism. Bad humanism sees value in humanity as a species. We can take pride in humanity's achievements as we also are humans. Sartre thinks this absurd for, as each person creates their own nature, I cannot take pride in what others have chosen independently of me. Good humanism is the view that humanity is 'self-surpassing', which simply means that as a person creates her own nature, she is always making more of herself than the being she was born as. A cow is a cow is a cow, but a person can choose for herself and thus transcend the being she once was. This is existential humanism, which puts humanity in control of itself, but as individuals, not as a species. With this point Sartre echoes his opening thoughts.

▶ Conclusion

The book began with three complaints against existentialism, that it implies quietism, solipsism, and ethical relativism. Has Sartre successfully seen these off? As to the first, I think Sartre has done a good job. Existentialism does not lead to inaction. In fact, it demands action of us, and shows us that even when we think we're just going with the flow, we have actually and actively chosen.

As to the second, Sartre's claim that the *cogito* implies intersubjectivity is not very well supported. But then we could question how important the *cogito* is to existentialism. After all, we are still condemned to be free, no matter where we stand on the debate over the *cogito* and certainty. In this sense, the best response to critics is not to refute the charge of solipsism, but to say that solipsism is a general philosophical problem, not an especial one for existentialism.

As to charges of relativism, Sartre's replies seem very weak. Unless there is at least one universal moral value, then no moral judgement can be universal. Instead, we would just have a battle of wills – what I think is right versus what you think is right. Maybe Sartre should have just bitten that particular bullet (as Nietzsche did) and tried to move on from there, instead of desperately trying to find something objective with which to defend himself. Sartre wanted to sketch out his existentialist ethics in this lecture, but the resulting picture does not escape the problem that for existentialists, how one chooses is more important than what one chooses.

Summary

The charges against existentialism are that it leads to **quietism**, **solipsism** and extreme moral **relativism**. One aim of *Existentialism and Humanism* is to rebut these charges. Existentialism and **humanism** both put humanity at the centre of our world-view, but existentialism does not have humanism's faith in the inevitable progress of humanity.

Existentialism can be summarised in the slogan: 'existence precedes essence'. We have no creator and therefore we have no preordained purpose or function. Rather, it is up to us to carve our own destinies. In this way, Sartre's brand of existentialism is based on the non-existence of God.

The emphasis on the individual gives **subjectivity** an important role in existentialist thought. But this does not lead to solipsism because Sartre argues that when we choose for ourselves, we choose for everyone.

When we realise that we are fully responsible for our own choices, we feel **anguish**: This is inevitable, even though some flee from it or disguise it. This anguish is a result of our feeling of **abandonment**, the fact that we are alone in the universe, with no God, no universal values and no determinism; just ourselves, our consciences and our freedom to choose.

This means we must feel a particular kind of **despair**, since we cannot rest our hopes on the actions of others, or even that our own projects will succeed. We must forge our own values and it is in our acts rather than our words that we reveal our true feelings.

There are some ways in which we are linked to others. In some way, being conscious ourselves, we are directly aware of others as conscious beings too. We also share with our fellow humans the **human condition**: the objective limits on what humans can do. This contrasts with **human nature**, which is undetermined and free.

Sartre is thus able to repel some accusations levelled at existentialism. It is not true that it doesn't matter what we do, because with freedom comes complete responsibility. We can judge others because if they act in **bad faith**, they are denying their own freedom and the freedom of humankind. And existentialist values are real values because we can only have values if they are freely chosen.

Glossary

Abandonment   The state humans find themselves in when they realise that there is no God, no universal values or any other higher reality or truth to guide them.

Anguish   The fear or *angst* that grips us when we realise that we are entirely responsible for our lives and the moral values we choose.

Bad faith   When someone denies their own freedom and pretends that their actions are determined or constrained by external forces or higher values.

Despair   The feeling one gets when one realises that one cannot rely on others, humanity or any other inevitability that what we value will prevail.

Essence   The essential, fixed nature of a thing as determined by its creator. Sartre denies humans have an essence.

The human condition   Those features of human existence which we share with others and which provide objective limits to our actions, such as the need to eat.

Human nature   Humanity's fixed essence, which Sartre denies we have.

Humanism   The optimistic belief in the potential for humanity to progress without God.

Quietism   The belief that there is no point in doing anything since nothing we can do can change anything.

Relativism   The view that there is no universal standard for truth (epistemological relativism) or morality (moral relativism).

Solipsism   The view that the only certain reality is my own existence and that the existence of everything else is no more than probable.

Subjectivity   The way in which the world appears from the point of view of a particular, conscious being.

Further reading

Existentialism and Humanism, translated by Philip Mairet, is published by Methuen.

A good route into Sartre's other works is *Jean-Paul Sartre: Basic Writings* by Stephen Priest (Routledge). If you want to get serious about your Sartre, you'll have to tackle *Being and Nothingess* (Routledge).

Iris Murdoch's book *Sartre* (Vintage) is still considered to be a classic introduction to his thought, while *Existentialism* by David E. Cooper (Blackwell) puts Sartre in the context of the wider existentialist movement.

Glossary

A glossary for each text is found at the end of each chapter. Here are a few more general philosophical terms that are found throughout the text.

A posteriori   Reasoned from experience.

A priori   Reasoned from first principles, the truth of which are not established by the evidence of experience.

Deduction   A form of reasoning where, if the premises are true, the conclusion must also be true.

Empiricism   The style or school of philosophy which takes as the starting point of knowledge the data of experience.

Epistemology   The branch of philosophy concerned with questions of knowledge and its foundations.

Existentialism   The style or school of philosophy which takes as its starting point the idea of the necessity for humans to choose their own values.

Induction   A form of reasoning that uses the experiences of the past or future as evidence for truths about the past, present or future that cannot be established by more direct means.

Ontology   An account or theory of being.

Premises   The starting points of arguments, from which conclusions are derived.

Rationalism   The style or school of philosophy which believes the most important and fundamental truths can be established by the correct operation of reason, without reference to experience.

Sound   An argument which is both valid and the premises of which are true.

Valid   A successful deductive argument where the truth of the conclusion does follow necessarily from the truth of the premises.

Further Reading

Suggestions for further reading are provided at the end of each chapter. Here are a few more general recommendations.

The companion volume to this book is *Philosophy: Key Themes* (Palgrave Macmillan). As you might guess, it adopts a similar approach but looks at the themes of knowledge, moral philosophy, philosophy of mind, philosophy of religion and political philosophy.

The Philosophers' Magazine, which I edit, is a quarterly aimed at general readers as well as professionals. Its website is www.philosophers.co.uk

The best single-volume reference book on the subject is the *Oxford Companion to Philosophy*, edited by Ted Honderich (Oxford University Press).

For more ways into classic texts, Nigel Warburton's *Philosophy: Basic Readings* (Routledge) is an excellent anthology.

The Philosopher's Toolkit, by Julian Baggini and Peter S. Fosl (Blackwell) is a comprehensive guide to the techniques of philosophical thinking and argument.

Index